LEGAL CONUNDRUMS

V S Mani

Michael Terence Publishing

First published in paperback by
Michael Terence Publishing in 2023
www.mtp.agency

Copyright © 2023 V S Mani

V S Mani has asserted the right to be identified as the
author of this work in accordance with the
Copyright, Designs and Patents Act 1988

ISBN 9781800945036

No part of this publication may be reproduced, stored in
a retrieval system, or transmitted, in any form or by
any means, electronic, mechanical, photocopying,
recording or otherwise, without the prior
permission of the publishers

Cover image
Simpson33
www.123rf.com

Cover design
Copyright © Michael Terence Publishing

The Author's Appeal to Readers

This is a fictional novel, not a romance, detective, or crime thriller. Just everyday life in a select community in London in the 50s and later.

Please do not apply current-day norms to people's behaviour as it would lead to a big disappointment.

Synopsis

This novel, *Legal Conundrums*, deals with a young aspiring lawyer wanting to serve the community by saving money by not going to courts when they have various disputes. He offers Free mediating and Counselling services at the start and proceeds with his Fee Service of Legal Consultancy. This unique approach leads him to earn enormous amounts of money but saves several times that amount to the clients.

He was able to support several youngsters in his practice and builds a good support unit. The cases handled were very varied his judgments were very fair to both parties.

As this story deals with legal issues and the need to deal with several specialists, where appropriate the procedures were listed in an Appendix and involved costs and charges listed in another Appendix. These need not be read except for most interested readers and the essence of the story could be followed.

The author concludes the novel when the pattern of daily activities was well established.

Contents

Prologue 1

1: Start of Legal Practice 3

2: Que Sera Sera 26

3: All Are Judged Finally 43

4: A Tragedy Waiting to Happen 69

5: Systematic Approach for Long-Term Stability 86

Prologue

It was a sunny morning in Calcutta in 1932, when the British were ruling India. Dr Harry Ayer entered the prestigious British Medical Centre in Harrington Street in the centre of what was the posh area of the city in those days. The clinic was on a par with any high-quality such establishment in London's Harley Street and catered mostly for the health needs of British people in India and the Far East. Dr Steve Granger was a well-known Cardiac surgeon, and his wife, Dr Angela, was an eminent Paediatrician. Both studied in Cambridge and got married in 1905 in London after they became consultants. Elizabeth, their only daughter, was born in 1907. She also studied medicine specializing in Obs. & Gynae. They all came to Calcutta to manage the clinic in 1930. Dr Ayer had lived in Leeds, and he specialized in General Medicine. He worked in a Harley Street Clinic in London for three years before coming to Calcutta in 1932 to join the clinic of Dr Granger, whose family was very impressed with his knowledge. His handsome looks also appealed to them. In 1934, Liz married Harry in Calcutta as they decided not to go to London for the wedding and miss the clinic appointments. They had a son in 1936, and they named him Arun. When Arun was two years old, they returned to London in 1938.

The Granger family took over a clinic on Harley Street due to the retirement of the Senior Doctor, and owner of the clinic. They bought a 6-bedroom house with all-American type mod-cons. Arun went to a local kindergarten, and a private school, and was an intelligent student. He did well in his studies but was not good at sports. He specialized in Law, did bar exams, and joined a famous law practice for five years. He was to open his private law firm with a small office in St. John's Wood close to his house.

All was not smooth sailing in the Granger family's life since returning to London in 1938. They were in contact with old friends, and all seemed well for a couple of years. One of Liz's medical friends, Jennifer Joyce, working in Leeds mentioned Harry being a womanizer, had made two nurses and three fellow students pregnant and cautioned her to watch him. Liz told Jennifer that in Calcutta, the opportunities were few. Liz heard a few adverse comments about his affairs in London, which he denied vehemently. In Harley Street, with several clinics close by, he regularly met several nurses and young medics. Slowly gossip turned to complaints. Due to colleagues and other doctors' criticism, he left to Oz. Liz divorced him in 1940, and he left when Arun was four years old. Liz, by deed poll, changed her surname to Granger, and she did the same for Arun.

1
Start of Legal Practice

Arun was always close to his mum and did not miss his dad. With a secure household full of grandparents, and mum's affection, Arun became a model son and did well in his studies. He was good-looking, but he never dated girls or had a girlfriend, regarding them as sisters. He also cautioned them against dating, going to clubs and bars, indulging in kissing, and taking drugs; some had their drinks spiked, leading to sex and rape. Pregnancy and venereal diseases became common. He met Sandra, a good-looking woman, during his law degree in 1959. She avoided, like Arun, going to parties or dances. He helped her with her college work. Her mother was a close friend of Liz, and her mum, Jennifer, was also a medic. Sandra was keen to be a paralegal in the law society. One day while Sandra visited Arun's house, they had a discussion.

"Arun, I have listened to you all these days about not going to parties," said Sandra, "but I have tremendous peer pressure. No one in the peer group has taken drugs or had their drinks spiked. Would our understanding and relationships be affected if I attended a few parties?"

"Sandra, I would advise you to follow your heart and peers and not worry about the consequences," he replied. "Do you realize you are pushing me to my limits?"

"Arun, I am, and you have not replied to my query."

"Sandra, would it matter if our relationship was affected? And what would your reaction be if it was? For example, would you stop going to parties?"

"I need to think carefully and decide," she said. "I cannot understand why you are so stubborn on these issues."

"I agree you want to go with your peers. However, I belong to the micro-sector of the minority who want to live the way they want to, not as the majority. Sandra, you are not compelled to follow my restrictions once you start going to parties. You would have a lot of help from your group to take care of you from now on. Sandra in western countries 'skin to skin' is not regarded as a sin. Girls, like pharmaceutical company salespeople, have started giving 'free samples of sex' before marriage and, in many cases, even after marriage. I would never condone that."

"Arun, I passed the exams because of your coaching. Now I might fail without your help."

"I would be lecturing each week in the college, and you could attend like other candidates. I decided to put effort into someone who empathizes with me all the way. Your mind had started wandering to enjoy parties; even if you change your mind, I am no longer interested in you. Even in paralegal training, you would have to seek outside companies. You are a very bright girl, and even without my help, you will have a rosy future."

"I am sorry for this sad ending," she said. "Goodbye, Arun. I am not sure you will find your dream girl in western countries."

"Marriage is not an essential criterion for living," he replied, "and I may spend my life as a bachelor. It is better to want something that one does not have than to have something one does not want. I am also sorry for this sudden ending precipitated by your pushing me to the limits. I am glad it was now rather than later!"

Sandra went home and told her mum about breaking her relationship with Arun. Her mum was far from happy as she felt Sandra's future in terms of marriage and career was so secure that she had blown blew it by precipitating a decision when his intentions were quite clear to all for several years. Arun told his mum and grandparents, and they were sorry about the breakup with Sandra, too. They commented that in the pond there was a lot of fish.

A couple of months later, Sandra's mum came to see Arun's mum; she was in tears and told how at one of the parties, the drinks of Sandra and her two friends were spiked, and three persons raped them. They did not want to report it to the police due to the stigma of humiliation from the community. So, she was asking for Arun's help.

"Aunty," he said, "it is difficult for any lawyer to take up the case as the girls cannot name the persons, and after so many days, it's difficult to establish where the incident took place. Generally, young girls and women should report on the day or night it happened, and they should not clean up the vaginal areas to enable a medical doctor to examine and test them for rape. Usually, a blood test would also reveal the drug used even though the effect would wear off in a few hours. Hence, the speed of reporting is crucial. Please find out whether they befriended new guys or opted to go to unfamiliar locations, as these are details to remember for the future, and to avoid similar experiences. These would come under lessons to learn. I am sorry for not being very helpful on this occasion."

Sandra's mum understood the difficulty of taking legal action but thanked Arun for his counsel and then left. A few weeks went by, and Liz had a lot of calls about seeking legal advice from Arun.

"Arun," she said, "please start your practice soon as you might get business from now on."

"I need all the three of you to advise," said Arun. "We have a vast open ground next to our house, and I want to build an office there, two stories with parking for eight vehicles. The builder/architect quoted six months to complete," he added, as he showed the drawings to them. "The estimated cost would be £60,000. I am negotiating a delayed payment, and I should know in two to three days."

"We love the office premises," said Grans, "and we would pay the total cost in a week. Arun, treat this as your inheritance, and enjoy it from now."

"Arun, please take their money," said Liz, "as their blessings for the new venture. Inform the architect about the total payment within a week and start the work."

Arun gave a hug to all of them, but he would treat it as Gran's loan, repayable in three years to satisfy the Tax Inspectors.

"I need another piece of advice from you three," he continued. "I did a specialist course on mediating and counselling, as these were pertinent to family law cases. In the case of divorces, separations, and children custody cases, I intend to offer the first three hours or part thereof consultation as FREE. I feel that most family cases are simple, but relationships erode with time. They all need legal opinions without incurring any charge. The legal costs in court cases and procedures confound them. My route would seem very friendly and focus on family welfare. They would come to me, rather than go to a court. My cases may not involve informing the Tax Authorities, Police, Citizens Advisory Bureaus, etc. Instead, I would give an instruction sheet listing all the benefits of dealing with me. However, I would state that for cases involving manslaughter, murder, or any crimes, euthanasia, fraud, etc., these cases would not be treated as confidential and information would be passed on to the police and other authorities as appropriate. I intend to charge after the FREE consultation £150 per hour session or part thereof."

"It is a brilliant strategy to attract business," beamed Grans, "and shows a caring legal advisor. We applaud you for that."

Liz hugged him with tears rolling down her cheeks and said how blessed she was to have such a wonderful son.

"Grandma," said Arun, "I want you to be my secretary to answer phone calls till I start earning enough. My calculations are as follows: allowing advertisement and other sundries as £2,000, a loan of £62,000 for three years at 5% interest per year, means £22,050 per year; which equates to £1,840 per month; about £460 per four-day, for four weeks per month; £115 per day. The repayment is achievable once business and contacts pick up. Now, I had to advertise, and I have included grandma's name as the receptionist!"

They all wished him luck, and he put the adverts in two national dailies, five local papers in London, Liverpool, Leeds, Birmingham, and Manchester, and in five trade journals. He cleverly put the office address c/o his mum's, as many might relate to his mum, and noticed the business. The advertisement costs amounted to £1,200, which was part of the loan from Grans. After two weeks, his grandma's phone was very busy, and she booked 16 appointments in two weeks for mediation and counseling services. She was so excited but darn tired! She blamed it on not working all these days but enjoyed every second of being busy.

Arun engaged a young audio typist in the afternoons for two hours, payable at £15 per hour.

His first assignment was on the following Monday morning at 10. The couple were from Maidenhead, married for two years, had no children, and wanted to divorce due to incompatibility. The young couple came on Monday at 10 to Arun's office. They went to the reception to enquire whether Mr Arun was free. The receptionist led them to his office and closed the door. Arun said he would tape the conversations for security purposes so that no one could deny any statements. They both agreed.

Arun shook hands and requested them to introduce themselves and state the issues.

"I am Natalie Baker, married to Rudolf two years ago, and we have no children. He did not want to have any children, and he wanted to pursue his travels and see the natural wonders. I wanted to pursue my painting business."

"With each one's view poles apart, what made you both decide on marriage?" asked Arun. "Was it infatuation as you both are so good-looking?"

"You are correct, but we realized our mistake after a year."

"Arun, it was nice of you to offer mediation and counseling sessions," said Rudolph, "but we were beyond that stage."

Arun said he had to terminate that FREE session. Any further discussion would be subject to his consultancy fee of £150 per hour or part thereof. Natalie wanted to proceed.

"What were you expecting please, let me know frankly?" said Arun.

"I want a divorce settlement of £1 million," replied Rudolph, "and I would sign the divorce papers immediately."

"Rudolf, I would have to ask you a few questions to get the total dimension of the issues," insisted Arun. "Natalie, may I have your comments, please?"

"I own a £2 million business, and my profit in the last two years does not amount to £25,000 in total. I have substantial loans from the bank, borrowing on my house worth £250,000. I felt a two-year relationship did not amount to what he was asking."

"Rudolf, please tell me about your income in the last two years?" asked Arun.

"I was not working, and she knew my status before the marriage."

"Rudolf, please tell me your skills and where you worked before meeting Natalie?"

"I never worked from 16 years of age and lived only on the dole."

"Did you help her in her business or contribute to house maintenance? These would impact the divorce settlement for you."

"I did not know anything about art and her business, and I did not have any money to pay her. She pays me £250 per month for my expenses, and I toured the world."

Arun said it was time to have a tea break, after which he would make his decision. So, they had tea and some snacks, scones with clotted cream and jam.

"I have decided to help you resolve the case with the least expense for both parties," announced Arun. "Generally, legal terms of divorce settlements are based on various factors, but in a simple case like yours, the marriage period taken is for ten years. On that basis, a profit of £25,000 for two years would correspond to a maximum of £2,500 for the divorce settlement. You had not contributed to the business or paid for living expenses but traveled using her generous monthly expense payments; you are not likely to pay for any loans or interests to Natalie. I would consider a cheap world ticket for £1,500 over six months, as advertised recently, with £1,000 for expenses being the maximum you could get if you took it to any court. I wait for your comments, Rudolf, before we close the discussion."

"I am very disappointed," replied Rudolf, "but can see your line of thinking in trying to be fair to both of us. I accept and hope the cheque can be given to me now."

Arun got Natalie to write a cheque for £2,500 to Rudolf Baker, as per the agreement.

"I will get a typed agreement based on our discussions," said Arun. "Rudolf, you should not start your world travel until you have signed the divorce papers, which will be ready tomorrow by 10. Once you sign the divorce papers for filing, I will issue the cheque to you but not today."

Rudolf reluctantly agreed.

Arun called the typist to come in, and collect the tape and he wanted six originals, two for each, signed by all three parties. Arun asked the girl to bring two typed invoices. The girl typed out the invoices and put the documents in a folded file.

The three of them signed the agreement. Rudolf then left to come the next day at 10. Natalie was so impressed with Arun and said his low fee of £500 for 3 hours of consulting and typing the divorce papers, was very good. She was worried she would have to pay £10,000 to £12,000 to Rudolf, but it was considerably less, only £3,000 and she thanked him. She also congratulated him on having his grandma in the reception with a 'good-looking chick' as an audio typist. His grandma and the girl heard Natali's comments and were delighted. They both complimented Natalie on her way out.

Arun gave £50 in a sealed envelope to the girl, who was called Prema Raman. He asked her to come whenever his grandma wanted her, and she agreed. She was pleased with the bonus payment. First, however, Arun wanted to know more about her.

"I am 24 years old," she replied, "and the only daughter of my nearly blind father of 65 years and my mother of 55 years. My parents worked as housekeepers, cooks, etc., for a wealthy businessman from India. He asked my dad to help in the factory for no extra income. Their payment was below the minimum wage. Due to fumes in the factory, my father could not see. The businessman told my dad to wash with cold running water instead of taking him to the hospital. From that time onwards, he started to go blind. My mother is his carer. Her work suffered. My parents had to leave their jobs. They got redundancy pay for three months, only £90 in total for both. We were destitute shortly after. When I was nearly 12 years old, an elderly Indian gentleman took pity on us and helped me study and finish my BA. I learned typing at 16 years and started earning some money to help my mum and dad. I do not have a regular job, and no one pays as generously as you, Mr. Arun, with a bonus.

"Where do you all live now?" asked Arun.

"In a rundown flat in Haringey for the last four months," replied Prema. "We left the big house after the person, our mentor, passed away. The house was put up for sale by his English daughter-in-law."

"Does the businessman still live here?"

"Yes, and he wanted to misbehave with me, offering a typing job, which our mentor advised me not to accept. I would have refused anyway."

"Please give me your address and his address," said Arun. "Let us go now to your place and bring you back to stay with us. You work for me, and I will pay £300 per month with NI, Pension, and other benefits paid. Alternatively, you can have your own company, which I would set up for you, and I would pay for work as and when I get it. My gran would always be with you."

"Prema, it is your lucky day," said Gran, "as my grandson's attention fell on you, your future is secure. Go and bring your parents. We have a separate flat – three-bedroomed, fully furnished. We would also take your dad to a top consultant soon. I am sure Arun would put a legal claim on the businessman and get a sizable compensation for you all."

With tears rolling down his cheeks, Prema hugged the grandma, and in traditional Indian custom, she touched her feet and put her hands over her head. Arun was very moved. She wanted to hug him, but he stopped her. She said sorry. Arun then went with her to her flat, and within 30 minutes, they packed and came to grandma's place. Steve, Angela, and Liz were happy to welcome them, and Prema's parents nearly wanted to touch the feet of everyone. Liz forbade them. They all had dinner by 7 pm and were in the lounge. Two carers for Prema's dad, from 6 to 2 pm and 2 to 10 pm, were appointed. The afternoon carer took Prema's dad to his room and onto his tilting bed.

"We were very indebted to you all for giving us royal treatment for us destitute people," said Neela. "Was it a mistaken identity, or do you all have a period of repentance? Whatever it is, we were very grateful, and we would never be able to repay it. I am older than my age due to caring for my husband. We were glad you have put in two carers each day to lighten my load. I salute you all."

"Please," said Liz, "think of my mum and Arun's help as something due for a well-deserved family. Prema helped Arun on his first day of business very efficiently. She is such a good-looking girl, very clever, obedient to all elders, related or not, and I pray she has a wonderful husband soon."

"It was my lucky day," said Prema. "I got the telephone call from the agency for the audio typing, and the rest is history, as they say. I am very grateful to Mr. Arun for his generous rates and bonus."

"Prema, please call me Arun from now on, except in front of clients."

"For this gesture, I have decided to take your offer for a monthly salary with National Insurance, pension, and other benefits, from whenever you want me to start."

"Thank you, Prema. Your salary is increased to £450 per month as you would be Assistant Receptionist from tomorrow, answering telephone calls instead of my grandma so that she is not overwhelmed with telephone calls. My grandpa would also work as an accountant for a monthly salary of £300, and his timings would be to suit his convenience."

Prema and grandpa were very grateful for the opportunity and income.

"Prema," continued Arun, "your work timings are five days a week, and for weekend or holiday work, you would be paid double time on a pro-rata basis. Grandma would work max four days a week, and some days, she might decide not to come. So, you would have to cover for her. For grandpa, it is his timings and no office hours for him."

"Arun," said Liz, "you have included the family in the business as office staff, and from today I regard Prema as one of our family. This family involvement would be perceived as a very stable relationship, and your clients would be pleased. Neela, I talked to one of my friends, Amanda, a specialist in optometrists and ophthalmology, and she agreed to see your husband, Ramesh, on Wednesday at 11 so that Prema could accompany you two. Our chauffeur or Arun could take you three."

The maid came to ask for any hot drinks before going to bed, but they all declined and went to bed by 9, as it was a long day for Prema and her parents.

Arun was up as usual in the morning by five and went jogging in the back garden, which was huge. He then had 20 minutes of yoga, and after a shower, he came down by 6.30 for coffee. Prema's mum was also up and brought her husband down with the carer from the morning shift. Neela told the carer that her husband had poor eyesight. He needed to feel his way to go to the bathroom. He could manage on his own once he knew where the facilities were. The carer agreed to remove chairs and tables that impeded his walk which he did after breakfast. Arun said to Prema the previous evening, that he would call her parents, uncle, and aunty from now on. He told aunty Neela about taking South Indian filtered coffee in a small tumbler and dabara. Neela was aware of his specifications, and he had sizzling hot coffee in a few minutes. Neela's husband thanked him for all their good fortune and the eye appointment on Wednesday. Arun told the uncle not to worry about it. Arun then went to his office. Prema came to his office at 7.15 with her coffee. After preliminaries, she wanted to talk to him frankly about herself.

"Arun, you have been our God's messenger for changing our lives. I have so far had a sheltered life, without any boyfriend or even a close girlfriend. I avoided male acquaintances due to dating, kissing, etc. What if I had soft feelings for you? If you are not interested, I would not raise this matter but do the job to your satisfaction."

"Thank you, Prema, for opening your heart to me. It is better to clarify at the beginning. There were three reasons I was reserved. Firstly, my family background, and secondly, I had an unwanted experience recently."

Arun gave his early family background, why he was very close to his mum and grans. He also told his experience with

Sandra and her prophecy about not finding a girl who had not given free samples of sex!

"I had not kissed Sandra or had any relationship with her. You turn up from nowhere into my life. Isn't that God's gift to me? The third reason is I should not take advantage of your destitute situation. Once you were all well off, and I got some compensation from your father's previous employer, then I meant to open my heart to you. I fell in love with you the moment you walked into my office, and it seems you were in love with me too. Why not seal our bond with a hug?"

She walked towards him, and they fell into a sweet embrace and hugged. Arun said he would like to tell his family before breakfast. Prema said the whole family was having coffee in the dining room.

In the dining room, he told both families that he had found his soulmate for life, and with their blessing, he would like to marry Prema. She endorsed those sentiments too. All elders were happy and the staff too. Arun gave a bonus to each employee £50. Neela made a sweet Kesari for all to taste with the good news. Liz said her dream had come true, and the grans wanted the wedding soon. She went to her room and brought a costly diamond necklace, which her mum and dad gave her on passing medical. She asked Prema to put it on, and Prema, with tears rolling down her cheeks, hugged Liz, Grans, and her parents. The elders decided to have a simple South Indian wedding followed by a Civil wedding. Prema agreed to get the booking for the Civil wedding on a Wednesday.

***

Tuesday morning, Arun was to see a couple regarding their separation agreement and facilities and custody for the child. He wanted all the family to be in the office to introduce the clients for a few minutes. Arun asked Prema whether she knew shorthand, and she said her speed was 80 words per minute. Arun wanted to go to the office by 9 for discussions. Once Arun and Prema were in the office Arun said to focus on business issues.

"Prema," said Arun, "you are not an employee as you are a partner in our business. Grandpa and I will teach you accounts. In six months, Grandpa and Grandma need to be released from office work to let them enjoy their retirements. I would transfer my bank current and savings accounts as a joint account, and I would ask the bank manager to send papers to enable you to sign the cheques from now on. You could have separate accounts which you only could sign. We had a business loan of £60,000 from grans, which is repayable in three years. From this morning, attend all interviews and meetings, which will be recorded. However, please use shorthand to note non-verbal communication in crucial discussions. There are a few books on non-verbal communications on the bookshelf."

Arun went ahead to read the comments made by grandma on the visitor's request for consultation and mediation. Prema found two books and started reading. She placed the orders with her mum for two filter coffees at 9.45 before the interview. Her mum brought it, and Prema took it to Arun.

The visitors came at 10. After introducing the whole family, including his mum, they entered the office. Prema also joined them after putting the phone answering service to call after two hours so that grandma was not disturbed. She said that she had put the recording tape machine on.

"Please introduce yourselves," said Arun, "and the reason for the visit. Prema, my secretary, who will become my wife in three weeks will be here during the whole interview. The tape recorder is on so that we do not contradict later about not saying certain things. These are highly confidential to the three of us and not meant for the Home Office, Police, or Income Tax Officials. The first hour of the meeting is free to set the scene for actual consultation after this meeting. I will give the charges later."

"I am Fiona Smith, married with a son of four years, fighting a custody battle with my husband, Tony Smith. We married 5 years ago in Swansea. Tony and I unofficially separated last year. My mum's parents own a jewelry store worth £50 million; my dad is managing it now. Tony had extra-marital affairs with his secretary two years ago, which he promised to end but was continuing."

"Tony, please update me on the present status and your real intentions?" said Arun. "Does your secretary like to look after your son, even for short periods?"

"I am very impressed with your family connections," replied Tony. It tells us you value family more, and, hence, your mediation and counseling service to avoid unnecessary litigation costs for both parties, which is commendable. I made an error two years ago with my secretary as we were working late and my child was always crying at home. I avoided going home. Once the affair started, she had a hold on me. She was not keen on looking after a child, and she would want me to give up the wife and the child. My job as a manager was in a company owned by her dad."

"Have your parents been involved with the child in the last four years?"

"I quarreled with my parents when I was in my teens," said Tony, "and they left for Oz about 15 years ago. They did not come to my wedding or send birthday cards for the grandson. They have not returned to the UK so far. I am their only son."

"Tony, how much was your monthly salary, and how much did you pay for house expenses and the boy's welfare? Did at any time Fiona ask you to pay any amount?"

"My salary was £600 per month, and as Fiona was rich, I did not pay anything. She did not ask for anything. Also, my secretary was a high-maintenance variety, and I hardly had £50 at the end of each month."

"Sad background about your parents really," said Arun, "and nothing there to swing your way even a little bit. I empathize with you in one way, but once you stray, there is usually no return to the original status in most cases. I also feel that your claim for custody is to get more money from Fiona. Please tell me how much you are expecting?"

"I feel I should get £25,000 as a divorce settlement."

"My sincere opinion is you would lose the custody battle as you were unfaithful to Fiona. I have all the details I need to end this counseling service, and I need your acceptance before proceeding to my legal consultancy, which is chargeable at £350 per hour or part thereof. It is time to have a tea break after both of you accept the end of counseling."

"I am happy to proceed with legal consultancy to get to a solution than go to court," said Fiona. "Even though I have money, I feel it is wasteful to spend on any court case. "

"I do not have money to take it to court," said Tony, "hence, I agreed to see you. Let us have a tea break and discuss."

After the tea break, they assembled again.

"We start the tape," said Arun, "and my charge is £350 per hour or part thereof. I will make it brief, and you will both have a chance to respond. It seems Fiona has the money to have a maid to look after the child and the boy dotes on her. Tony, you rarely spend time with the boy, and he still regards you as a stranger. I am viewing this from the boy's perspective. He would be more at home with Fiona than you, and the boy has maternal grandparents' affection too. Tony, in your case, your parents are not here to see their grandson. Considering all this, you are unlikely to get custody of the boy. Out of gratis, Fiona may pay £2,500 as a payment to you, once you sign the divorce papers tomorrow morning by 10. Now I would like to have your comments before we agree to proceed further."

"Arun," said Fiona, "you have made a practical assessment focussing on the boy rather than on any adults. I agree with your decision and the settlement figure. This decision is better than going through the court."

"I was expecting a higher figure," said Tony, "but Arun, you cleverly brought out the negative points on my side, which I cannot contest. I agree with your judgment as well."

"Fiona, please write out a cheque in favour of Tony Smith," said Arun, "so that my assistant can photocopy it and include bank details in the Divorce settlement agreement. She will take the tape and type out the agreement document in six originals; two originals for each of us to be signed tomorrow before giving the cheque to Tony. Tea and scones are available until the agreement documents are ready after typing."

After 50 minutes, Prema brought the agreements for signatures. All three signed all the copies, and each kept two for their records. Tony also signed a document for the receipt of the cheque and left.

"My invoice for three hours is £1,050," said Arun, "you have to give a cheque to us."

"Arun, my dad, was estimating a £10,000 payment," said Fiona, "but now it's only £3,550, which is a lot lower. I will preach your skills to my contacts so that they do not need to go to court for legal action. I will change my and my son's surname to my parent's surname, Fisher, by deed poll. She hugged Arun and Prema, thanked the grans and Arun's mum who had come early from the hospital, into the front office, and left.

"Arun, you paid a bonus to Prema yesterday but forgot today," said Grandma.

"As we are getting married soon, she is no longer an employee but will be my partner in the business, which is a mega bonus for her, grandma!"

"As an accountant," said Grandpa, "I saw your computations for £150 income per day to repay your debt. On the first two days, you had invoiced £1,550, an excellent start, grandson. Let it grow bigger from now on."

"Arun, your offering mediation and counseling as free was a great incentive for most family feud cases," said Liz, "and they would opt for the Free first step to appraise the situation. Also, surrounding yourself with the family as office staff would instill confidence in most cases for getting a very balanced judgment."

"I found out I had saved £6,000 and over on both days," replied Arun. "I increased my charges from £150 per hour or part thereof to £350 per hour, and for Prema's case with the businessman, I will increase it to £1,000 per hour. I will adjust my charges to each instance and for the affluent people I handle, I might charge £500 per hour or part thereof."

They all went for a nice samosa snack and filter coffee. After that, Arun agreed to take Prema and her parents for the eye appointment. Liz said they should all be optimistic.

The evening dinner was quite simple, and the cook started following Prema's mum's instructions. The Granger family liked vegetarian food only while in Calcutta. Arun excused himself and went to the office to prepare for Thursday's visit by a newly wedded couple regarding alimony payments and Prema's dad's compensation claim. Prema came to help him by bringing her folders. She closed the office door, and they both hugged for a while. Arun saw her dad's monthly salary payments over twenty years, including the recent factory work with no salary received. He also took details about the businessman asking Prema to work in his company as a typist to misuse her, which never materialized. After a further few minutes of discussions, they left the office and went to their bedrooms.

The next day, Arun left with Prema and her parents after her mum recited a long prayer invoking all the Gods to restore Ramesh's eyesight. They reached the eye clinic quite early, and the consultant took them to her room after asking the secretary not to put any telephone calls through for the next two hours. She explained AMD, (Age-related macular degeneration). She said it occurs in all persons above 50 years, and it has two types, dry and wet. Anti-VEGF medicines – ranibizumab (Lucentis), aflibercept (Eylea) and brolucizumab (Beovu**),** were prescribed. She explained that:

Injections are given directly into the eyes:

- stops vision getting worse in 9 out of 10 people and improves vision in 3 out of 10 people
- usually given every 1, 2, or 3 months for as long as necessary
- drops numb the eyes before treatment – most people have minimal discomfort
- The effects of the treatment included bleeding in the eye, feeling like there's something in the eye, redness, and irritation of the eye.

She stressed it could take four to five visits with repeated checks to detect any improvements. She then asked them to leave the office and the nurse to get tea and biscuits in the waiting cubicle.

Arun and Prema left to go to the Council registrar's office to confirm their Civil ceremony in two weeks on a Wednesday. The lady at the counter gave them forms to complete and made a provisional booking. If the completed forms were delivered by 4 pm that day, the booking would be confirmed in writing. Civil wedding to be held at

11.30 and would take 30 mins followed by the issue of wedding certificate after signed by two witnesses. She stressed the hall had a small capacity for 20 visitors, excluding the bride and groom and two witnesses. The doors would be closed by 11.30, and anyone arriving late would miss the ceremony. She laid down the rules very clearly, and emphatically. Prema paid a £30 fee and £100 for the council fund for charity. The lady thanked her for her charitable contribution and wished them a long and prosperous married life. They returned within an hour, and her mum was saying slokas peacefully.

Prema had all the documents like passports, birth certificates, and driving licenses. Next, she completed the forms, including the parent's wedding certificate details. Arun checked after completion and signed where relevant. Then, as the nurse said it could take another hour at least, they went to the Council offices to deliver the forms, and after 30 minutes, collected the confirmed booking letter and returned to the clinic.

The consultant came out by 11.30 and said it was promising and she had not found any need to give the injection. She gave her an appointment for the following Wednesday. She wanted the patient not to overdo it by watching TV or reading books, even with large print. Arun and Prema invited her to their civil wedding in two weeks. She wished them a happy life and would talk to his mum in the evening. Prema then paid £250 fees and took the receipt. They returned home in time for lunch. Her mum joined them to get the latest news which Prema told crisply. She also showed the letter for the Civil wedding. Neela had cooked in the morning for 8 for lunch. They had a sumptuous lunch, and grans and Prema's parents went for a siesta. Liz rushed back to the surgery. Arun and Prema went back to their office for prepare for the next day's legal meeting. Before that, Prema closed the door and gave a huge hug to Arun. They were in that excited state for a few minutes and reluctantly separated.

A telephone call came, and Prema answered. It was from a landlord in Haringey wanting to evict some students, who had refused to pay rent for over three months. Arun took the call, explaining his business and qualification to handle landlord cases as well, and he agreed to mediate and counsel to avoid expensive court costs. The landlord was quite happy, and Arun offered the following Saturday, starting at 10, which was readily accepted. Prema was impressed with the expansion of legal cases and working on Saturdays. Arun said the motto should be "chase the money," like Goddess Lakshmi, when she comes, never refuse! Prema agreed smilingly.

He prepared the compensation case for Prema's dad and drafted a long letter about proceeding with the legal claim in court. He explained his business strategy offering mediation and counseling for three hours for free. After that, he would proceed with the legal claim in his office to avoid expensive court costs, exposure to Tax Authorities for incorrect staff payments and in some cases for non-payment, and even the accountant for colluding to be sent to prison. Prema typed the letter and demanded a hug for fighting for her family. Arun made it a short one, and he wanted to focus on the alimony case.

2
Que Sera Sera

Arun came to the office at 7, and Prema joined at 7.15. Her mum brought hot filtered coffee by 7.40, which they enjoyed, and looked through the notes. Grans joined at 8.45. The couple came at 9, and Prema introduced them to the family. They entered the office, and she introduced Arun as her boss. Arun said he expected his PA always to attend the meeting. Prema suggested tea or coffee now or after a few hours. However, they wanted to proceed ASAP. Arun asked them to introduce themselves.

"I am Sally Trotter, 26 years old, married three years ago. We have two boys, a 2-year-old and a one-year-old. I was working in a Tesco supermarket as a counter girl. I do not work now as the boys take up much of my time. I have no interest in sex these days, which caused friction between us. Jim started having affairs with his office secretary for the last two years. As a result, he applied for a divorce, which is proceeding. Jim was to pay monthly alimony on filing for the divorce. He is a multimillionaire owning five large houses and two petrol stations. I will answer more questions as we proceed."

"It was a sad case," said Arun. "Sally, what was your income, savings, and parental support, if any?"

"I get £40 a week per child from the family support unit. I have savings of only £100. I do not get any parental support as they died twenty years ago. I have no siblings and no relations. I moved from one adopted parent to another. I did not smoke, drink, or take drugs. I was a good student but poor. I was good at singing and was teaching young children and earning a small amount. I was in the Anglican church choir.

"The church took pity on me and helped me. I passed the "O" and "A" levels. I was good at audio typing, where the money was good, but I did not get regular assignments. So, I joined Tesco at 19 years, and one day I fell for the sweet-talking Jim when he bought a few things in the shop. It led to marriage. Jim was 40 years old, and many in the church advised me not to rush.

"Nevertheless, I fell for his wealth and thought God had finally given me an escape route. He treated me well, but I got pregnant within six months, and it was the end of our romance. My church friends used to give me a small amount of money. They mostly gave used clothes, prams, toys, and items useful for the kids."

"Many thanks, Sally," said Arun. "Please, Jim, tell me your side highlighting your wealth, monthly income, and business loans. How much do you contribute monthly to Sally for her property rent and children's expenses?"

"Arun," replied Jim, "I am impressed with your family support in your legal office. My wealth would be £20 million, but all tied in loans. I have a monthly rental income of £6,000, but the outgoings relating to the property are £2,500. My income is £600,000 a year from the two petrol stations. The profit after expenses is £40,000. My bank loan is £11 million at 5% interest. I do not contribute anything to Sally as I felt she tricked me into having both children without taking adequate precautions. Also, I felt she had a boyfriend in the church group."

"How long did both of you live together?" asked Arun, "and when did Sally move out of your house?"

"I drove her out after six months when I felt she tricked me and became pregnant."

"How much did you pay her monthly for her expenses? And was it adequate to buy family planning tablets?"

"£20 per month. I thought she would have got those tablets from the NHS."

"Where did Sally move to?" asked Arun, "and did you check the accommodation?"

"I was so furious; I didn't care where she went and stayed."

"Did you ever visit her in the flat, to see the child after it was born?"

"I saw the child in the hospital and refused to go to the flat."

"Did you think of putting her in one of your nice, heated houses? Should you be considering that from now on?"

"Not really, my property value would go down. As for the future, let me think."

"Is there anything else you want me to consider before I say on this aspect of mediation and counseling?" asked Arun.

"Nothing else from my side," replied Jim.

"And nothing else from my side," added Sally.

"Your alimony payment issue is an example for couples to know about and avoid in their case," said Arun. "There are five strategies used:

Strategy 1: Avoid Paying It in the First Place.

Strategy 2: Prove Your Spouse Was Adulterous.

Strategy 3: Change Up Your Lifestyle.

Strategy 4: End the Marriage ASAP.

Strategy 5: Keep Tabs on Your Spouse's Relationship.

"Jim, you have attempted to use Strategies 1 and 2, though not effectively in 2. As you have not said anything for 3, 4, and 5, I will ignore the issues about those. These will not become a factor in your defence. In a court, a judge would consider the following factors: the standard of living of both parties; Jim, you had a very high standard, whereas Sally was destitute. Time Married. Three years is too short a period. Condition of Both Parties. Same as before marriage. Sally had to provide for two young children and from charity payments from the Anglican Church. Financial Resources. Jim, yours is very high and dependable. Sally is touching the poverty level. Professional Capacity. Jim, you are a businessman, whereas Sally is a young girl, and you have taken advantage of her. Individual Contributions to the Marriage. Jim, you would have borne the simple marriage expenses. Future Parenting Responsibilities. Jim, you have exhibited no parental responsibilities so far after fathering them two years ago. Sally had taken good care of them as any devout mother would do. Tax Implications. So far, none to you as you have not paid any money to affect your tax situation. However, not paying under these circumstances could result in hefty penalties and a prison sentence.

"I have analysed your situation carefully, and now the Free mediation and Counselling part is over. Therefore, unless you two have anything to say, I will close this Free session and proceed to the legal consultancy."

"I am happy to hear your judgment on this issue," said Sally.

"Arun," started Jim, "you have very cleverly listed the issues as a court would consider. Please proceed to the next stage."

"Now we move to the legal judgment area," said Arun, "and it is not free. Jim, you wanted the meeting, and you have the finance to pay and not Sally. My charges are £500 per hour and part thereof. I am focussing on the welfare of the children only. Jim, you have stated that she tricked you and had two children. No jury in any country would agree with you. Any court can sentence you to prison. By not paying Sally, you are starving the children, which would further the term of the sentence. You have a high monthly income of over £4,000. I have computed that Sally should receive £850 monthly. Of this, £500 is for looking after the toddlers, £250 per month for the rental and other related heating, and electricity, and £100 for kindergarten, which should start in a year. Sally reported that her landlord had cut off electricity and water in her written disposition as she did not pay rent for these for three months. She notified you, but you ignored it. I can raise all these issues with the local council, the landlord for irresponsible behaviour, and the tax office for auditing your business accounts for the last three years. I have computed a figure of 30 x 850 = £25,500 for all the arrears for 30 months. Also, you should always pay in advance for six months £5,100, making a total of £30,600.

"The advance payments would be going through me for you to escape a lot of penalties and possible prison sentences. I would also put in 6% for a rise in costs each year. If you agree with my judgment, I will get this agreement typed, and you would route the six-month advance payment through my bank account, and the penalties for defaulting would be very severe. The advance payment would be a legal document enforceable by courts. If you agree, Jim, I will get this typed by tomorrow for you to sign but please issue cheques for the two amounts now in favour of Sally Trotter. My charge will be for three hours, which is £1,500. Jim, please issue a cheque for my company."

Prema prepared the invoice for £1,500 and gave two copies for Jim to sign. After getting his signature, she kept one copy and gave the other to Jim. Jim gave her a cheque for £1,500 and the other two to her. Jim then left. Prema gave both to Sally and asked her to go to the bank immediately, as it was only 3 pm. Prema said she wanted to see the bank credit slips ASAP. Sally went, and in 40 minutes, she returned and showed Prema the credit slip. She wanted to thank the family before leaving. She said thank you to the grans, Liz, who had come early, Prema, and Arun.

"Arun, I am so happy that you made me a human being again," she said, "deserving of some consideration and respect. I never dreamt about this much money. Jim was in the bank and said I could move into one of his ground-floor flats with no rent or service costs to pay as he would bear it. He was not worried about future payments as he felt the children and I deserved it. The removal people will come at 10 am tomorrow and complete the move by mid-day. It had all security outside the compound and in the flat. A maid will come to help me, and he did not want me to seek any employment as children needed full attention. I could teach students to sing and be in the church choir. I saw an immense transformation, and it is due to your persuasive presentations and forceful arguments. By highlighting his weaknesses, you strengthened my case, and you always focussed on the toddlers. That was your strength and trump cards. I take you as my brother from now on."

"As you were an audio typist, please type some documents for us. The hourly rate is £10 or part thereof. We would pay £15.00. Would you be interested? Please ask Jim to agree and contact Prema from now on as she would be your boss."

"I used to be an audio typist before I joined Tesco," said Sally. "Your office is only 10 minute's walk from our new flat. As I have a maid, I would come for two hours max, to do the typing. I will ask Jim and confirm tomorrow.

"Sally, you should bring the two boys one day," said Liz.

Sally agreed and left.

"Arun, you are a wily fox," smiled Grandpa. "I admire your skills and strategy. We will read the various discussions and learn several things from you."

"We will have Sally type the documents," said Arun, "as Prema will be busy with me in the meetings."

"Arun, you are well ahead of your income forecast," said Grandpa.

"From tomorrow, I will charge £600 per hour or part thereof. For Prema's dad's compensation, my fixed fee will be £10,000. The businessman will save ten or more times this amount by not going to court."

"Good luck to you and Prema, your partner in business and life!" Grans and Liz joined in their wishes for him.

The elders went to the house, but Arun stayed on for the next day's appointment details. Prema joined him in the office, closed the door, and they had a long embrace and hug. She thanked him for asking Sally to do the typing, and she said they would need one for typing the agreement each of the four days after the meeting. Arun told her that Sally would do that, as she could bring the children with the nanny here to look after them. Prema was impressed with his planning and decided to leave him to all recruitment. At that time, he had a call from Sally that Jim had agreed to her working.

"Sally, you start working for our AP Legal Consultancy Limited on Monday. Your monthly salary will be £500, with NI. 10% company contribution to your pension, 4 weeks holiday. You will have a joining bonus of £1,000 on Monday. Please report to your boss, Prema, my PA now, but my wife in two weeks' time. She will tell you the working hours each day."

Sally replied like a shot, and Jim agreed immediately.

When she was in the office, Sally said the meeting with Arun and his family was the best thing that had happened to her. Arun reminded her it was years after her meeting, Jim who gave her all the free flat and the two lovely boys earlier. She smilingly agreed.

Prema was astounded by the speed at which Arun was planning and deciding for her benefit. Arun said she needed a new receptionist to answer calls during working hours. She felt having another audio-typist would be beneficial as well. Arun said they would get candidates soon, in a matter of days. They went through the messages and found out the next day's couple was wealthy, middle-aged, and wanting to separate. The wife wanted to walk out, but the husband was using threats to stop her. Arun wanted to read about it and follow case laws. Prema went home. The evening dinner was peaceful, and they went to the lounge for chats.

"Ramesh," asked Liz, "how do you feel today after the first eye appointment?"

"I am happy to see much better than all these days. If after the next appointment, my eyesight is better, then I would not need the carers. I did not watch TV or read any books. Frankly, both are not my usual pursuits. Listening to the radio or music on religious tapes are my pastimes. I am glad to hear about the wedding date and times confirmed. Liz, we are blessed to have a family like you to pick Prema for your son, Arun."

"We should say that both are blessed to get each other," she smiled.

"Ramesh," said Neela, "you had a long, exciting day, and you should go to sleep giving rest to your eyes. It applies to all of us too."

They all agreed and went to their bedrooms.

The next day, an elderly couple came at 9, and Prema introduced them to the family. The maid brought coffee and biscuits. This hospitality pleased them and they were impressed by how the three medical doctors were helping the family business. Prema took them to the meeting room, introducing herself as PA to her boss, Arun.

"We were pained to hear about separation at this age," said Arun. "When you both should be helping the family and grandchildren. I started this Free mediation and counselling session to make the individuals rethink and compromise. After this session, for legal advice and judgment, my fee would be £4,000. You may find the legal and court costs would be several times higher, and all would come to know of your quarrels and problems. In this case, it would remain confidential. Please give us some background; Prema has put the recorder on since we entered the room."

"I am Dorothy Compton, married to Dennis for nearly 30 years. We have a married son with a grandson and a granddaughter living near us, and a daughter married with two granddaughters, 21 and 18, living close by. In the last three years, Dennis has become bossy and interferes with everything. I used to be Head of Personnel Management in a medium-sized company with 50 employees. Now I feel treated like an idiot, a good-for-nothing individual. Nevertheless, I have my savings of over £1 Million and lead a quiet life advising companies from time to time."

"It is sad to hear your comments and how hurt and lonely you must feel," said Arun. "I need to ask you several questions. Let me give you a few minutes to think, and I'd like Dennis to introduce himself to us."

"I am impressed with your family's support for your business," said Dennis. "Your grans helping you puts us to shame and I wish we had avoided this meeting. I would willingly pay your fee, which is a tenth of what it would have cost us if we went to court. We heard a lot about you, Arun, and the importance of family, and we chose to see you. I had my company trading in the stock market and was doing very well. Our family wealth is £25Million. My son looks after the company. Our daughter-in-law is a Cambridge Ph.D. in finance, and she has her own Financial Services company. The grandson, Jack, is good at Maths; he is 22 and works as an actuarial at Standard Life Assurance Company. My granddaughter, Diana, is not good in studies but good as MC in all the functions and wants to work as a receptionist. She did not like the small company she works for as the boss wants to misbehave. Our daughter has two daughters, Tara, and Stella, both working."

"I am interrupting to give you some information on my Grans, mum, and me," said Arun. "Prema, my PA and I are getting married in two weeks and please come. Prema, all our cases teach us something valuable. After 30 years, we should never be like this couple. I am sorry to say this, but you are unlike my grans, by giving importance to yourselves, you ignore the others, mostly youngsters. There is a receptionist job here, and Diana can start tomorrow. Tell her to resign from that company of the pervert immediately. I am astonished Dorothy, with so much Personnel Management experience, you were not guiding your granddaughter, and she might have lost her way due to perverts under your watch."

Just then, they heard a commotion in the reception room. Prema and Arun stepped out and saw two young girls wanting to see their grandparents. Prema took them to the meeting room, and the girls hugged their grans and requested not to separate. It was an emotional scene, and they were all crying.

"Please take a seat and calm down," said Arun. "Were you supposed to be at work?"

"We both work in a small firm recommended by my grandad," replied Tara. "The boss, 40 years old is a randy sob. He wanted me to go for a weekend with him to Brighton. He was always chasing Stella to have a hug and kiss. We were afraid he would try to have sex with me. Because he was a friend of Grandpa, we were in a quandary. Mum and dad were too busy, and Grandma had her battles with Grandpa. We did not want them to separate as we would be all alone."

"Please, both of you resign now," said Arun. "I will send a special courier with my letter to your boss in an hour. I want all of you to be quiet when I talk to Tara and then Stella. Tara, please tell me about yourself, your qualifications, and what you like to do."

"I passed Management Accountancy," she replied, "via BBC Open University for three years, and I was first. I did not want to study for a while as I wanted to earn and learn. My salary is £150 a month without NI or pension, etc. I am a temporary employee for six months, with three months more to complete."

"Are you good at dealing with Tax Office, NI office, Pension section, etc? Could you fill in the relevant forms for each employee and manage monthly salary accounts for each staff? Will you be confidential at not revealing individual details of each employee and operating the filing system?"

"These are what I trained for, and I would be happy to do these."

"You start working for our AP Legal Consultancy Limited on Monday," said Arun. "Your monthly salary will be £750, with NI. 10% company contribution to your pension, 4 weeks holiday. You will have a joining bonus of £1,000 on Monday. Please report to your boss, Prema, my PA now but my wife in two weeks' time."

"I am delighted to work for you with a super salary package. May I hug you, please?"

"Hugging will be the downfall of all women. Learn to do a Namaste, the Indian way," he said and showed her. "Now, I'd like to talk to Stella. Tell me about yourself, your education, jobs and what you like to do?"

"I am not a good student, but I learned audio typing. I am happy meeting and talking to people and am good with children. My present salary as a typist is £100. I am a temporary employee for six months with two months left to complete."

"Stella, you can start on Monday as an audio-typist, and the salary package is as follows: Monthly salary of £500 with NI, 10% pension contribution by our company, 4 weeks annual holiday. You will have a starting bonus of £1,000 on Monday. Prema will be your boss."

Stella did a Namaste to Arun and all and thanked Arun and her new boss. Just then, a young girl came to the reception. Prema brought her to the meeting room. She introduced herself as Diana.

"Diana, you start working for our AP Legal Consultancy Limited on Monday," said Arun. "Your monthly salary will be £500, with NI. 10% company contribution to your pension, 4 weeks holiday. You will have a joining bonus of £1,000 on Monday. Please report to your boss, Prema, my PA now but my wife in two weeks. Tara and Stella, please wait in the reception office. We will all have lunch here, and we will join you shortly."

He returned to Dorothy and Dennis.

"Due to my new business, Dorothy, and Dennis, I was conservative in stating my charges to you both. I should have charged you £10,000, my usual consultancy fee. I do not think we need to go to a further assessment by me. You both will have learned your lessons and decided to work together as grandparents to look after the grandchildren."

"Too true," said Dennis. "We learned several lessons from you. The way you dealt with my granddaughters, gave them jobs at high salaries with perks, and how you handled the rogue on their behalf was all praiseworthy. I decided to pay you £12,000 as your fee for advising us and saving our granddaughters."

"Thank you, Dennis," said Arun, "and please see the letter to your friend. Let us all have lunch now."

There was a big party for lunch including Sally, her nanny, and the two toddlers. And, of course, all the guests knew that cooking would be vegetarian only.

Arun read them his letter to Tara and Stella's employer

"Dear Sir, I am enclosing the resignation letters of both girls,

Tara Fisher and Stella Fisher. Both are temporary employees and had not completed six months. It appears in both their cases, you had tried to take advantage of the young girls by wanting to hug and kiss them, and in the case of Tara, you wanted her to go with you to Brighton for a weekend. They came to me, and as you were a friend of Mr Dennis Compton, I am taking this matter not to threaten you. What you tried to do is unethical and immoral.

Please see some details regarding illegal types of harassment. These include harassment due to race, age, sex, religion, national origin, colour, disability, pregnancy, genetic information, illegal activity, taking Family and Medical Leave, and making a worker's compensation claim.

You have harassed them due to their age and sex, explicitly or by insinuation. As a result, you subjected them to severe stress and mental agony.

You should be careful about asking young girls for frequent hugs and wanting to kiss them and take weekend visits to hotels with a view to sexual and immoral purposes.

Please send a letter of apology to each of them for your bad conduct.

Pay an outstanding salary and, say, a penalty payment of £1,000 as compensation for such behaviour to both employees. I expect a reply with salary and compensation within a week of receiving this letter, which is sent by a special courier today.

One could report to you to Company House, the local employment ombudsman, etc. However, we do not want to precipitate actions that would lead you to a long custodial or prison sentence and even loss of the company.

I await your reply, ASAP.

With kind regards,

Arun Granger.

Arun then asked Prema to get this letter typed on AP Legal Consultancy Ltd letterhead and addressed to their employer; Mr. Dennis and Mrs. Dorothy Compton, Tara, and Stella to approve. Input from Dorothy might be more appropriate, and she could add or delete as she chose.

Prema was careful that as Personnel Management Head, she should make sure the facts and accusations were correct. The draft was to be checked by all. Once agreed, Arun signed, and the signed resignation letters of Tara and Stella were enclosed and all sent by courier. Dennis had a copy.

Prema efficiently handled the whole job by asking Sally to type the letter,

Stella for audio-typing the meeting from the recorder, and Diana answering the phone. Tara wanted to start immediately. Arun asked her to check the calculations he had made for daily income. He wanted Prema to learn accounting basics. He told them that the monthly salaries amounted to:

Tara £750

Stella £500

Diana £500

Sally £500

Arun £2,500

Prema £2,000

Grandpa £300

Grandma £200

Total Salaries for 8 £7,250

Total working days 22

Income needed/day £330

Payment to cover the loan £150

Total income needed/day £480

Income earned: £500+£1,050+£1,500+£12,000

= £14,100 in 4 days (=£3,525)

"Arun," said Grandpa, "you are scaling new heights. Now you have eight staff to manage. Do not forget the invitation to people coming to the Civil wedding, catering in the hall and the house, flowers, bonus payments to staff, and staff lunch in a hotel."

"It's all arranged," said Prema, "and invitations are verbal only due to a shortage of time."

She told Arun about the simple layout of the accounts and the healthier state the business was in.

"Let us focus on the case on Saturday between the landlord and the students," said Arun.

As they were still in the office, Arun hugged her for bonus income from the elderly couple and Prema for getting three assistants to her by having three new employees. Then, they went to the dining hall to join the others.

3
All Are Judged Finally

On Saturday at 10, the local council representative came with the three students to contest the case. Prema offered tea and biscuits, which the students enjoyed, but the representative refused and looked grumpy. Saturday was the usual day off for all staff, but Sally, Tara, Stella, and Diana came to work, saying they would move the extra mile for such a caring and considerate employer. They all refused double rates for Saturday. The visitors were quite impressed with this employer-staff relationship. Prema said she was PA to her boss Arun.

"I must thank all of you for taking the trouble to come today," he said. "The Council representative knows that I specialize in family law. I am also qualified in other areas. I offer a free mediation and counseling service, and after that period, I charge a fee. The Tenancy Act and the various issues are very complex and involve legal experts fighting in the courts. It means spending thousands of pounds and taking a long time. Today, we discuss and agree within a few hours and get on with our routine life. Most of the cases are easily solvable with a common-sense approach. I would like you to introduce yourself first and present your case."

Prema had put a recorder on to tape the conversations from the moment they entered the room.

"I represent the Council," said the Representative, "which has let flats to the students. The Council rental agreement states: how much was the rent; what it included whom to pay; when to pay; how to increase the rent.

"The tenants had written agreements. They defaulted for the last three months, and it amounts to £150 per tenant. The total amount outstanding is £450."

"I request one of the tenants to summarize the issues," said Arun.

"We are second-year students doing Finance, commerce, and other disciplines," said Student A. "We were following Earn and Learn. The factory we worked for on late evenings, closed, and there were no suitably paid jobs. The factory might reopen in two months. We will be in arrears for six months each, totaling £900. We will pay £90 monthly, taking twelve months to pay off, including the interest. Our studies are affected. No parental help in each case, unfortunately. We did not want to borrow on credit cards and pay 21% interest. I have nothing more to report."

"Representative, would you like to say something?"

"I have nothing to say now, Arun."

"Will you students, give me your grades, please?"

"We are grade 2-1 type students," replied Student A. "We never failed but got grade-1 in some subjects."

"I am pleased to hear about your grades," said Arun, "and hope it does not get lower due to rental problems with the Council. I have enough information from both sides to conclude this Free session. From now on, it is chargeable. My charge is £4,000, and if this is acceptable, Representative, I have something else to say to benefit both parties."

"Compared to court costs and time, Arun, you have wrapped up in less than an hour. I agree to the charges and will issue a check now."

"Thank you, Representative. Please, give me a cheque as per our invoice for £3,000 only. Retain £1,000 as payment on behalf of the students for the amount overdue with interest. You are all invited to a vegetarian lunch which will be ready shortly."

"I must applaud you, Arun," said the Representative, "for sticking with family values and helping the students. I will praise your laurels to other Councils not to waste their money on court cases."

The students went and hugged Arun and thanked him. Then, they accepted the lunch invitation. Prema felt the attraction was the girls in the reception. The Representative thanked them for the lunch invitation but declined as he had to do some shopping with the family.

Prema brought the invoice - two copies for the Representative and Arun to sign. The Representative gave the cheque for £3,000 to Prema and left. Arun and the group went to the reception, and the students never missed Arun, Prema, or the family till they had lunch and left. Neela gave the girls and students packed food for the evening. The students tried to chat up the girls, but Prema told them sternly that no meeting in the college or club, dancing, kissing, drinking, etc. allowed.

"Please focus on your studies to get good grades," she told the students, and then she sent them back to their flats. They left reluctantly.

"Arun, it was very nice of you to help the students and the Council," said Grandpa. "I am sure other councils and tenants will love you for it."

"All is not rosy, Grandpa," replied Arun. "One of the disgruntled husbands has reported me to the SRA - Solicitors Regulators Association and the Legal Ombudsman for unfair awards. The Ombudsman considers cases when SRA is unable to deal with them. The husband should contact me first before going to SRA, but he bypassed me.

"The procedures are: If the person has complained to the solicitor about breaching the SRA Code of Conduct and is not satisfied with the response, he can report them to the SRA. Solicitors must follow the code of conduct. Examples of a breach include dishonesty, fraud, and discrimination.

"If one has complained to your solicitor about poor service and is not satisfied with their response, one can contact the Legal Ombudsman. The Legal Ombudsman deals with poor services, such as delayed or unclear communication; problems with your bill; loss of documents.

"Prema, please prepare folders for all cases as we go along. Folder for Invoices and payment receipts; folder for Income, expenses, profit, or loss;

folder for staff salaries and deductions, bonuses, etc; folder for Staff Contracts of Employment."

"Do you know who it is?" asked Grandpa.

"I am asking a few people, I also asked Natalie."

"I know it is my husband," said Natalie. "He never earned a penny till now, and he has a friend who provoked him to get more money from me. This SRA route is to get some more money by discrediting Arun. I will not let that happen."

"It is nice of you, Natalie," said Arun. "This complaint might take a few weeks before I need to reply, so let us not get agitated now. Please ignore the issue. Prema, when SRA or Legal Ombudsman deals with a case, we need to send only the case details and relevant information. The folders must be always for viewing by Grans and us and must be kept in locked cupboards only."

"Do you have any contacts in the hierarchy of both organizations to get feedback?" asked Prema.

"Prema, you are brilliant. I do not have contacts there. My mentor who was at the University does. I will talk to him and send all the cases for comments. Please get one copy ready by Monday to send by courier to him. I will contact him now."

Arun called and his mentor was available to talk. Arun explained his strategy and the cases he had handled so far. He invited him to the wedding, but he declined, as he was giving a lecture in Edinburgh. He wished both a happy married life. His mentor wanted the case details sent by courier immediately. Arun said he had set up a new company. He would send as a token £500 for his comments. His mentor thanked him. Arun told Prema and others that his mentor would send the comments by the middle of next week. His mentor was the advisor to several legal establishments.

Arun went to the office, and the elders, including his mum, went for a siesta. Prema joined Arun in the office and closed the door. They hugged for a long time, and she told him the gesture of paying the outstanding rent was classy!

Arun said they should focus on the claim for compensation for her dad. He drafted a strongly worded letter, seeking fair payment of outstanding salaries for Ramesh and Neela. The claims listed non-payment of even minimum hourly rate, national insurance, and pension benefits for both, injury to Ramesh while working in a toxic fume environment, instant termination of employment with a pittance of an amount for over 40 years of loyal service to him and his family. There was also another issue of enticing his young daughter to work for him and yield to his sexual advances. He wanted to see the accountant and the company records for the last 40 years, listing all monthly salary payments and registering with Tax Inspectors.

He sent in his company letterhead and included the FREE mediation and counseling service, followed by his appraisal and judgment for the case which was chargeable. The advantage of this route was the low cost of legal fees, and no court fees, including expensive lawyer fees. Also, all discussions were confidential and not reported to any influential external bodies, Tax Authorities, The Company House, Ombudsman, Police, etc. His fee for all the above was £20,000. Arun stressed that the business might incur massive costs if it went to court. An investigation by the Tax Office for non-compliance, their auditing of company records, arresting of the accountant followed by a prison sentence. As the Director, he might be stripped of his position, and all assets and sent to prison. Arun stressed that the businessman might not want to face those hardships. Arun said he would wait for the phone call from the businessman to discuss the next stage for this issue.

Prema read the draft of the letter and agreed. She typed the letter and sent it by courier immediately. She then asked whether the charges were high. Arun laughed and agreed. He said,

"If one compared his actual court costs, investigations, two possible prison sentences, his dignity, etc., he would opt for my charges. On that day, you were to be absent. I will have Grandma sit with me in the discussions. Once he pays the cheques for your dad and me, after depositing in the bank and seeing the credit slips, I might introduce you. I am not sure about it now. Prema said she was not keen to see him ever."

They returned to the dining room for coffee and samosas.

Arun came to the office to check the appointments for next week. On Monday, a young professional couple decided to divorce and there was a conflict about splitting the property. They had two young children and a custody battle also loomed. Arun was looking at some old cases and judgments made by the judges. The wife is English, but the husband is Scottish.

Arun made some notes: it is usual for tempers to flare during a custody battle, as your emotions usually were running high. However, having a verbal or physical altercation with the other parent could and would be used against one in a custody battle.

Fathers lose custody because of child abuse or neglect, substance abuse, exposing the children to overnight guests, or not following the right of first refusal agreement. Child abuse is the number one reason a parent loses custody of their children.

The difference between English and Scottish law? Both Scotland and England are part of the UK, but Scotland has a separate judicial system and jurisdiction. Therefore, rather than being solely a Common Law system, Scottish law is a mixed system, and one should be aware of the differences.

Do mothers have more rights than fathers in the UK? Fathers do have the same parental rights as mothers. However, in the UK, a mum automatically obtains parental responsibility once her child is born, but the situation is more complicated for the dad.

Arun returned to the dining room, and after a simple dinner, they went to the lounge for the usual summing-up discussions.

"Arun," said Grandma, "you were big-hearted in giving the outstanding rent to the students, thereby removing pressure from the Council. When did you plan to do it?"

"As the meeting progressed," he replied, "I was impressed that their grades were 2.1. They were under stress during exams. I felt their rent was more important than my profit."

"Arun," said Ramesh, "I am happy that you are claiming compensation on my behalf. Prema briefed me on that. Good luck to you and me." He then went upstairs to lie down and listen to some classical songs.

"Any updates, Arun?" asked Liz.

Arun told her about the divorce and custody case of a young professional couple. The mother is English, and the father is Scottish. A tricky one. Then he mentioned his mentor and awaited his comments on the cases.

"Roll on Monday. I plan to charge them £5,000 as both are professional, high-income-earning couples."

Liz wished him good hunting!

On Monday morning, Arun had a call at 7.30 from his mentor, who told him that he had written the most complimentary letter for dealings by Arun and judgment being honest, fair, and correct. Arun asked him to send his letter by a courier, who would collect it within an hour with all costs paid by him. Arun was very excited and told the family. Prema was very relieved. He had a call from the businessman wanting a meeting on Wednesday. Arun agreed to the date.

At 10, a young and smart-looking couple came to the reception, and Diana introduced the staff, and the family and offered coffee which they enjoyed. Later, she took them to the meeting room and introduced Arun and Prema. She said that she would record the discussions and put the tape on.

"I request that you both introduce yourselves and the issue involved. Let us start with the Lady first, please."

"I am Florence Denyer and was married to Barnaby Jones for nearly four years. We have two daughters, Christy, three, and Georgina, one. We are a highly skilled professional couple, and each of us is too devoted to our work. I manage a recruitment consultancy agency and do headhunting for large companies. I do not travel out of London, but he works out of London and the UK. He wanted a divorce and filed a suit. So, I changed all our surnames to my family surname by deed poll. I will stop now for Barnaby to respond."

"Thanks, Florence," said Arun. "Your initial statement opens a can of worms for me. I will come back to you later."

"I work for a steel manufacturing company," said Barnaby. "Europe is where most of my consultancy work was. I rarely stay in London. We both had a strong outlook, and we were results-driven. Out of frustration for not being able to talk amicably, I filed for divorce without consulting her. I regret it, but it is too late."

"I'd like to understand the divorce issue," said Arun. "Barnaby, do you prefer to withdraw the divorce suit? If yes, please let me know. What else do you want to rethink on your marital issues? When did you file for divorce? Also, to ask a very personal question of working late nights in far-off places, have you had sexual relationships with women and been unfaithful to Florence?"

"I fly off the handle most of the time," said Barnaby, "and I regret that. My plea to her is to listen when I shout but ignore all of it in a few minutes. I filed for divorce about eight months ago, but she knew about it only two months ago. I did have a few one-night stands in the hotels I stayed at."

"I understand your predicament," replied Arun, "but as an intelligent person, you should agree that no self-respecting person, even a wife, would put up with this request of listening to a verbal tirade, especially when she had gone off at a tangent. Her not knowing about filing for divorce for six months is a monumental mistake on your part. Also, being unfaithful to her would work against you in any litigation. I understand you wanted to raise custody issues. What is your monthly salary, including bonuses? How much do you pay Florence for family maintenance, rent, utilities, etc.? How many hours do you spend with the children in the week, and how much are your wealth and assets?"

"My salary was £5,000 and I get paid a £12,000 bonus for each year. So, my monthly salary is £6,000. I am worth £6M. My parents own about £20M. Both my parents are in good health. I did not pay anything for maintenance, rent, food, etc., as Florence never asked for it. I never offered as well. I save

£100 a month for each of the girls to be payable on reaching 16. I had not told Florence. I hardly spend any time with them."

"I am astounded to get your salary and wealth details," said Arun. "I'd like to focus on Florence now. How much are your salary, wealth, and assets? Have you been unfaithful to your husband, and if so, when did it start, and is it continuing? Did you know about his infidelity, and how long ago was that?"

"My monthly salary is £3,000, and I do not get any bonus. My saving is £25,000, and my investment is £15,000. My parents are retired schoolteachers owning a house worth £600,000. I have a younger sister in her final year at university, doing Finance. I never had any extra-marital relationships. I never knew about his infidelities as those happened abroad. I never asked for any money as I felt he should know about his responsibilities as a dad. After three years of marriage, we never discussed his wealth, and I only came to know now."

"I have a good understanding of the issues involved," said Arun. "It is time to end the FREE session, and I will start my judgment. If you both agree, I shall proceed."

"I agree that you could start," replied Florence.

"I also agree," added Barnaby.

"Now, my charge for the judgment of your tragic case is £6,000. Barnaby, with your wealth, you should pay for it, and Florence need not pay anything. There are several mistakes that you have made. Your behavior shows you did not even know your commitments to a family and children. Taking your share of expenses as 50%, you did not pay for food and living expenses amounting to £1,200 per month; heat, electricity, utilities, etc., £200 per month; mortgage expenses of £200 per month; child maintenance of £150 per month; services of the maid £50 per month; holiday or other events expenses of £100 per month. In effect, you left Florence to pay £1,900 for nearly two years, amounting to £45,600. The fact that you did not tell Florence about the divorce application for six months might be due to vengeance, which is inexcusable.

"You had not been with the toddlers in the evenings or night to read bedtime stories; you might not have any experience of dealing with toddlers; you were not concerned about your absence, and you were not planning to make changes to your job to accommodate the toddlers in your life; you also cheated on Florence many times. With your frequent travels abroad, you are unlikely to change. In my judgment, she is unlikely to reconsider the divorce you filed. So, you were hoping against hope! All these would go against you in case of seeking custody ever. So, it is a total non-starter for you. One of the reasons fathers lose custody battles is for child abuse or neglect, and in your case, it is neglect.

"I will instruct you to pay in advance for expenses for six months £11,400 to my bank account, and any default will be deemed punishable by the police and might lead to a prison sentence. A 6% increase in inflation per year was budgeted. In my judgment, please issue three cheques, one to Florence for £45,600, and one to me for my charge of £6,000. and the third cheque as an advance payment of for six months £1,400. My assistant will give you, my invoice. She will also get the judgment typed giving the details of the three cheques. Any comments from either of you?"

"I am pleased with your summary, and I have nothing else to say," replied Florence.

"Arun, you have addressed all the key issues and listed my negative points," said Barnaby. "I apologize for being so bad. Now I understand I have lost her and the children for good and forever. I had enough money, and I should have paid her. I will write the cheques now."

The three parties signed the typed Agreement and took two copies. Then, Diana went to the bank with the details and brought the credit slips.

Barnaby left, saying goodbye to the staff in the reception. Florence was very excited to get a substantial sum which she never expected, and she told Arun in a way she felt relieved to get Barnaby out of her hair. She met the staff and thanked them all.

"Florence, what does your sister plan for work?" asked Arun.

"She is good at stock market trading. I will ask her to come now as she is at home, ten minutes away."

"Please ask her to join us for lunch," said Arun.

"Tracy will join us in ten minutes," she said.

Tracy came and Arun wanted to talk to her with Prema for a few minutes before joining them for lunch. The rest went for lunch.

"Tracy, please tell me about yourself and what you would like to do?" he asked.

"I am 20 years old and have just finished my final year at the university. I had a project on stock market trading and got the top award. I would like to be independent and work on trading. Would you be able to help me, please?"

"You will achieve your dream now. We set up a stock trading company with you as the Director, and Tara, our young accountant, as the Company Secretary. You and four youngsters, working for Prema, are in this office. Prema will tell you some ground rules of behavior for you all."

"Tracy, you are a university student," said Prema. "We deplore activities leading to any dating, boyfriends, parties, drinking, or snorting drugs leading to rapes and pregnancies. We operate as a family unit and all should behave accordingly."

"Tracy, the rule for trading is as below," said Arun. "As self-employed, you will receive a loan of £1,000 from me, for one year only. No interest is due. You should pay Tara after the first year £250 monthly. You pay your NI, Pension, tax deductions, etc., which Tara will set up. All in the family will invest with you, and your commission is 10%. However, those in the office, including your boss and Tara, will invest monthly a portion of their salary for buying upmarket company stocks as savings for the long term. You can charge 5% interest only. You may charge up to 50% and progressively reduce it to 20% as you see fit for other investors. All losses are to your client accounts only. If you decide to operate from an outside office and not here, then our investments with you would cease instantly. Tracy, I have said my piece, what are your reactions to the proposals?"

"Boss," replied Tracy, "am I allowed to hug you both for the best news I have had in my life?"

Prema allowed a gentle hug to Arun but no kisses. Smiling, Tracy hugged them, and they went for lunch. Tracy gave them the good news and Florence hugged Arun, but Tracy stopped her kissing, saying it was not allowed by her boss, Prema. Liz said that Tara's role was increasing by the day, and she was happy. After lunch, Arun, Prema, and Tracy went to the office and opened an account with Barclays Stockbrokers Ltd. Also, they registered Tracy Denyer Stockbroker Ltd., with The Company House.

Tara informed the Tax Office about Tracy Denyer operating a Limited company as a self-employed for Stock market operation. Arun said that it would take five to seven working days to complete all formalities. He told her to go to the office, read the newspapers such as the Financial Times and Trade Journals regularly, study the stock market, and make meticulous notes on price changes. Tracy said that Arun made her think like a professional in a few hours. She then left for home after taking a copy of the Financial Times to read.

When the two were alone, Prema was looking for a hug, and Arun responded.

"Prema," he said, "you are only a year older than Tara; do you feel you are getting married at too young an age?"

"Not really, Arun, I feel I should have married you three weeks ago!"

Arun hugged Prema and wanted to see the booking for the next day. It was a complex case of a young couple with two children involving child custody, a paternity suit, and a protection order against domestic violence. Arun said he had to read a lot and make notes to help the next day.

The Family Court and Family Division deal with all kinds of legal disputes with children and the breakdown of relationships. Most seriously, the Family Court will deal with cases where the government (local councils, in practice) intervenes in a family to protect children from harm. 1 in 4 women are survivors of rape or sexual abuse and 8 million are women in the UK.

"All our services are free," he said. "With an experience of rape or sexual abuse, people react to traumatic events in all manner of complex ways, and they may feel fear, shame, anger, disgust, guilt, numbness, have nightmares or flashbacks."

Arun and Prema joined the others for dinner. After a simple dinner and sweets, they met in the lounge for discussions.

"What is the case for tomorrow, son?" asked Liz.

"It is a complex case," he replied, "involving a not-so-young couple with two young daughters, 5 and 3 years. It appears to be a concoction of lawsuits. The husband filed a paternity suit, probably thinking the daughters were not his; the wife filed a child molestation suit and a protection order against domestic violence. I had to go to the office, pick up some files, and read about old cases with the judgment given."

To lighten the mood, he mentioned his talk with Prema about marriage.

"Prema, you are only a year older than Tara, and do you feel you are getting married at too young an age?"

"Not really, Arun, I feel I should have married you three weeks ago!"

They all had a good laugh.

"Mum, I must say that we had found gold dust in employing Sally, Tara, Stella, Diana, and Tracy. Each one is brilliant and belies their ages with their mature performances.

Tara is the queen pin of my business, and Tracy will take our wealth to another dimension soon."

"You have been good in talent spotting," said Grandpa, "including Prema. You have an efficient youthful team and your mentor is to be applauded for his letter."

"Tomorrow will be another busy day," said Neela, "and we all should go to bed."

They agreed. Arun got his notes and went to his bedroom too.

In the morning, a couple came at 10, and Diane greeted them, introduced the family members and offered coffee, which they welcomed. Then, she took them to the meeting room, introduced Arun, and Prema, and turned on the recorder tape.

"We are delighted to meet you both," said Arun. "Please, introduce yourself, and give an idea of the issue. But before that, I'd like to say a few things. I understand that Stan contacted us, and I expect payment from him for my charges. There are three cases for discussion, including child molestation, protection against domestic violence, and paternity. After a 3-hour FREE mediation and counseling session, I usually charge £6,000 per case, but I will charge £18,000 for the concoction of the three. Again, I expect to receive payment from Stan. Stan, if you disagree with the charge, please let me know before we proceed."

"Please proceed, Arun," he said.

"Emma, please proceed."

"I am Emma Jones, married to Stan for six years. We have two daughters, Megan, 5, and Isla, 3. I filed two cases against

Stan for child molestation and protection against domestic violence. When you ask questions, I shall clarify. I am from a middle-income family. My parents, schoolteachers, are now retired. I am their only daughter. I used to help in the school kitchen before marriage. Since marriage, a housewife. My savings in the bank are £800. I have no investments. I get some money each week from the government for the two children. Stan allocates £200 for my monthly expenses, including childcare, toys, etc. My friends in the school canteen give their old toys and clothes to the two girls. I do not have a car to drive and use the old, worn-out pram to go to the school about a mile away, rain or shine."

"I am sorry to hear that, Emma," said Arun. "I have several questions to ask you, and the Free session may exceed three hours, which I do not mind. I will switch to Stan for now."

"I am a property developer," said Stan. "I own ten houses and two commercial properties. I earn monthly from these properties £75,000 and expenses £35,000. I buy run-down properties, renovate, and in six to ten months sell them for £300,000 to £500,000 or more. My property and business yearly turnover of £6M, and I draw a notional monthly salary of £5,000. I own two cars, a Jaguar, and a Porsche. I used to have a Toyota estate for Emma and the kids, but I sold it two years ago. My final wealth will be £30M."

"What an entrepreneur you are," said Arun, "everything you seem to touch turns to gold! I am astounded that with this wealth, you treat Emma like a slave and pay £200 for monthly expenses, including for the two daughters. Why is it, Stan?"

"I filed a paternity suit because I feel the daughters are not mine. Emma must have had an affair, and the children must have been born out of wedlock."

"With so many workers under you, you did not track her movements or visitors to your house. It is surprising to me. Did you employ a private investigator, and if you did, what did he report to you?"

"It was an expensive exercise, and he said there was no one. I started suspecting him too. I had another private investigator, and it was a blank too. I suspected Emma had affairs with them, and they lied to protect her."

"Stan," said Arun, "you did not for a moment suspect you could be paranoid about her having affairs with any man she meets? She takes two children in an old pram to school, walks one mile, and returns home, making food and then picking them up from school at 3 pm and bringing them home, giving them food, etc. When do you think she has time to have affairs?"

"I wanted paternity tests to prove they were not mine. She was refusing tests."

"I understand her unwillingness as she never had extra-marital relationships. Stan, people, do paternity tests before the baby is born or soon after birth. To test after three to four years is difficult to prove. Did you have any candidates who would agree to the tests? If not, yours is a meaningless dream. In my opinion, experienced lawyers would throw it out of court. According to world statistics, between 14 and 30 percent of paternity claims are fraudulent."

"I cannot name anyone now," replied Stan.

"Now, I turn to the next case, protection against domestic violence.

Emma, please let me know why you sought this protection?"

"Stan gets extremely angry and resorts to violently beating the children and me till we turn blue."

"Did you report to any neighbour or GP as soon as it occurred?" asked Arun.

"Yes, and the GP saw the marks on my face, hands, and back. She also saw the black bruises and scratches on the skin. She wrote to me about reporting to Social Services. I requested her not to do it as Stan might murder us. But she went ahead, and they questioned Stan. He told them that I was a chronic alcoholic and beat them regularly. Unfortunately, his work schedule prevented him from being at home to witness the beatings. I do not drink as I am a teetotaller."

"Did the GP ever test you for alcohol abuse?"

"Every time I went, she found the tests negative. She had permission from the police and NHS to use a breathalyser."

"I am asking for personal details," said Arun, "as these pieces of information affect the case. Has Stan ever been involved in sexual relationships against your wishes?"

"He usually comes very late and drunk. He forces himself on me even when the children are sleeping with me. He throws the children to the other bed, and he will have sexual intercourse despite my objections. Their crying does not distract him. He would beat me severely till I yielded. I reported to my GP, but she said it was an area she could not help with. Unless there was photographic evidence, she said that I had to file a suit, which was what I did."

"Emma, the experience of rape or sexual abuse: people react to traumatic events in all manner of complex ways, and you may feel fear, shame, anger, disgust, guilt, numbness, and have nightmares or flashbacks. Have you felt some or all of these?"

"I experienced all of it. I am glad you are asking several aspects meticulously."

"Stan, now I am going to deal with child molestation. I need to understand the existence, extent, frequency of occurrence, and proof of your legal case. Child sexual abuse includes a touching and non-touching activities. Some examples of touching activity include touching the genitals of a child or private parts for sexual pleasure; make a child deal with other deplorable acts. Some examples of non-touching activity include showing pornography to a child; deliberately exposing an adult's genitals to a child; photographing a child in sexual poses; encouraging a child to watch or hear sexual acts; inappropriately watching a child undress or use the bathroom. Emma, please tell me when you suspected child abuse?"

"About two years ago, he started suspecting they were not his children."

"Did you have any adverse comments about Stan's sexual inclinations?"

"He admitted that he had misbehaved with young boys."

"Interesting though your comments might be," said Arun, "these were not legally valid. He could deny saying that to you ever. So, I am going to ignore the comments. Did the GP check the children for any abuse in any parts of their bodies?"

"She noted injuries around both their vaginas, and she took photographs and informed the Social Services. They put the restraint order."

"I saw those, and I will deal with Stan. Let us take a break for vegetarian lunch?"

They all agreed and had lunch delivered to the kitchen in the office block. They did not meet any of the reception staff. After 30 minutes, they returned to the meeting room.

"Stan," said Arun, "you are in a very delicate area, but apart from the GP and Social Service involvement, you did not have a legal case to defend. However, whether you had relationships with young boys or girls, now or in the distant past, I must caution that as you are talking to a lawyer, the seriousness of the allegations means checks made by the police, school, councils, etc."

"The way you have phrased it, I am trapped. I was on a paedophile list for some years. Police told me that I was out of the list," replied Stan.

"It means Emma saying you told her some years ago, was true."

"Yes."

"Did you interfere with the girls because you thought they were not your daughters?" asked Arun.

"I never remember interfering with them, even though I do not regard them as my children."

"How do you think their vaginal areas with severe injuries happened?"

"I am not an expert on bodily injuries."

"Stan, before the children were born, did you and Emma visit pubs for dinner, etc.?"

"Many times."

"What drinks did Emma fancy in those days?"

"She was a misery, and even in good, friendly company, she would not drink alcohol. Only fruit juices."

"When did you both stop going out?"

"Before the children were born."

"She never tasted alcohol?"

"Not to my knowledge."

"It is four hours and 30 minutes of "Free" session of discussions," said Arun. "Now, I will start my 'fee' session unless you both want to say something?"

"I have nothing to say," replied Emma.

"I also have nothing to say," added Stan. "You can give your judgment."

"Emma, it was nice meeting you," said Arun, "but sad; it was not under pleasant circumstances. You have shown considerable mental strength and resolve in bringing up the two daughters with a belligerent husband. A lot of your experiences did not have supportive evidence.

"Stan, it is not common to see such a wealthy businessman in our office. However, managing a £30M empire is no easy task, and it must have its pressures and pleasures. I have my conclusions as follows:

a. Paternity lawsuit - you were paranoid that Emma had a lover. You had subjected her to a lot of stress, physical and mental, by selling her car, and pushing her to walk a mile each way to school, rain, or shine, twice a day. You gave her a pittance of money for running the house and care of the kids. You told lies to the GP and Social Services about her being alcoholic when you admitted to me that she did not drink when you took her to pubs. You admitted being a paedophile and molested young boys and girls. You denied molesting your daughters and injuring their vaginal areas. You abused your wife by having sexual relations when she refused, tantamount to rape. You were violent and beat her up frequently, causing injuries to her, and denied them to the GP and Social Services.

"The agreements of the GP, Social Services, and a lawyer is enough for the police to act against you. These would amount to you being in prison and losing your business. On referring her to a psychologist who confirmed mental and physical stress would amount to thousands of pounds sterling in compensation.

"In my judgment, you are guilty on all three counts: a wrong paternity suit, guilty of physical violence to wife and two young kids, and guilty of child molestation.

"I recommend that you pay Emma £3M to allow her a legal separation. There is no empirical formula for these cases. The simple calculation is like this: a wife gets 50% of the estate after 20 years of marriage. As you were married for four years, 20% is the share and of that 10% is only for her. So, for your wealth of £30M, she should get £3M. Also, you should not contact her ever. You could agree to pay in instalments over a year, but you should pay her £100,000 now. A balance of £2,900,000 should be paid over the next ten months at £290,000 monthly. You must also issue a cheque to me for £18,000 now. I will have these payment agreements typed, and after our signatures, we have copies. The instalment payments are legally binding, and any default would mean immediate arrest by the police. I am sure you would not want a hassle with the police. I await your comments, Stan."

"What if I refuse?"

"All conversations have been on tape," replied Arun, "and these would be sent to The Company House, Tax Authorities, The police, Social Services, and other public bodies, etc., by tomorrow by special courier. Your empire crumbling is imminent, and your prison life would be a lot sooner than you think."

"I will issue cheques to Emma and you. For Emma, the first instalment is just now, and will plan for the next ten months' payments."

Prema arranged to get an invoice for £18,000 and gave copies to Stan. Diana got the cheques for Arun and Emma, and they both went to the bank to deposit and came back in 30 minutes with credit slips. Stan then left murmuring, "Good riddance."

Emma hugged Arun, but Prema said no kisses, as she was marrying him in a week. Arun invited her to the wedding. He suggested arranging for a maid to look after the kids. She agreed and promised to pay £20,000 as a 'bonus' to Arun for getting her a fortune. She also asked Arun to help her manage the money. He said his accountant, Tara, would do it, and she should buy a car so that the maid could drive to school and take and bring back the children for her mum to test and check as she is a medical consultant in the hospital. Prema invited her for that evening dinner with the kids, and their chauffeur would pick her up at 6.30 pm. She agreed and left in a taxi.

Arun, Prema, with the reception staff met for tea as Neela made samosas, cakes, and filtered coffee. Liz came early from work. Arun told them that he had a bumper income, £18,000 plus a bonus of £20,000 to come. He told Tara to prepare some statements from the account books of Prema for the case against the businessman. He said she had to work most of the night to finish it!

4

A Tragedy Waiting to Happen

Arun asked every staff member, grandma, grandpa, and his mum to come for breakfast at 7 am as he had several things to say about the day's case. After breakfast and coffee, they all went to his office.

"Today's case deals with Prema's dad's compensation claim," said Arun. "She will be at home with her parents and not come to the office. No one should talk to them till the meeting is over, and we return home for coffee. I need grandma to be with me at the meeting. Diana, you receive the visitors, introduce people at the reception; after coffee, bring them to the meeting room, introduce us and inform them, and switch on the tape recorder. Grandpa, Tracy, Tara, Sally, Stella, and you stay at the reception."

"Arun is something worrying you?" asked Grandma.

"I sent him a strongly worded letter and sought a large compensation claim," replied Arun. "He will defend his methods and agree to disagree. It might slowly build up into a tug-of-war between him and me. He might refuse to pay anything, and at that point, I would have to threaten him. On the other hand, something good might come out of this. I would get my fees and payment to all my staff for several months of investigatory work."

Liz wished him good luck.

The visitors, four of them, came at 9. Diana met them and followed Arun's instructions. After coffee, they went to the meeting room and met Grandma and Arun. She told them about putting the tape recorder on.

"I am delighted to see you all," said Arun. "Please introduce yourself to us before I say a few words."

"I have come with my daughter's friend, Mia, the present accountant, as the earlier one was unwell for a couple of days, and Peter, a young lawyer," said the Businessman. "I am busy and want the issue wrapped up, one way or the other, in a couple of hours."

"I will try to meet your needs, Sir. We have two new people here. I will have to make my case clear to them. I am seeking fair payment of outstanding salaries for Ramesh and Neela. The claims listed non-payment of even minimum hourly rate, national insurance, and pension benefits for both, injury to Ramesh while working in a toxic fume environment, instant termination of employment with a pittance of an amount for over 40 years of loyal service to him, and his family. There was also another issue of enticing his young daughter to work for him and yield to his sexual advances. I wanted to see the accountant and the company records for the last 40 years, listing all monthly salary payments and details registered with Tax Inspectors.

"My meeting has the FREE mediation and counseling service, followed by my appraisal and judgment for the case, which was chargeable. The advantage of this route was the low cost of legal fees, and no court fees, including expensive lawyer fees. Also, all discussions are confidential and not reported to any influential external bodies, Tax Authorities,

The Company House, Ombudsman, Police, etc. My fee for all the above is £25,000."

Arun stressed that the business might incur massive costs if it went to court. An investigation by the Tax Office for non-compliance, their auditing of company records, and arresting of the accountant followed by a prison sentence. As the Director, he might be stripped of his position and all assets and sent to prison. Arun stressed that the businessman might not want to face those hardships.

"My accountant had prepared payment details they received from the company and shortfalls. In addition, she had listed the missing documents for the 40 years. The claim amounts to £45,000 for Ramesh and £25,000 for Neela. The unpaid pension payment from Tax Authorities rules for both is £30,000. Ramesh is seeing an eye specialist. Her fee is £250 per visit. He might need another nine visits to recover most of his sight. That would be £3,000. So, the compensation claim for both amounts to £103,000.

"You tried to entice their young underage daughter, 15 years, to work for you for sexual gratification purposes, and day-by-day details till she refused and fled her house was given for your support group to see. For that hurt, she is claiming £5,000."

Arun gave them a copy of all the calculations and said it was better to have a coffee break to study the report. After 30 minutes,

"I'd like to have individual opinions from each of you, starting with the lady first."

"I came in to join the group only two days ago," replied Mia, "and I was not involved in any of these. I need at least a week to understand and form a definitive opinion."

"Mia's comments apply to me as well," said Peter. "However, I have not seen anything legally wrong in these claims."

The businessman was so annoyed he fired Mia and Peter on the spot. They wanted to leave the meeting, but Arun requested them to stay on for a few minutes as the meeting might come to an unsatisfactory end.

"We were sad that the two, in their budding careers, had lost their jobs dramatically. I await your comments, Sir," said Arun.

"The world is full of crooks," said the Businessman, "including you and the eye consultant bumping the fees. Ramesh and Neela were nothing till I brought them to this country. I gave them food and a roof over their heads, and they were ungrateful. That daughter is a loose character, and all the details concocted to extract money from me, Arun's typical trait. I will not pay a penny and will fight it in the courts. All your threats about my losing wealth and going to prison do not frighten me. You can go to hell. The Tax Authorities only screw money from hard-working people like me.

"I am not disappointed in you disagreeing but using accusatory language on all of us, and even the Tax authorities confound me. Would you please retract what you said?" demanded Arun.

"Never!"

Arun said he had no option but to send all details, including a copy of the recorded tape to the Tax Authorities, The

Company House, etc., within 72 hours. The meeting terminated, and Arun and Grandma left the room. The three discussed for about fifteen minutes, but the youngsters got more scolded. Finally, they left without saying goodbye to the reception staff.

Arun and grandma decided to have coffee with Prema and her parents. Grandma asked the rest to listen to the tape, and they did just that. They came back and were stunned by the vitriolic comments of the businessman. Arun asked them to calm down. Tara was annoyed at the accusations and said Mia was her classmate and a very bright student. She was a snob and was friendly with the businessman's daughter. She was sad about Mia getting fired and asked whether she could work for her. Arun told her it was risky to get her to work now, but we should see how the issue develops in a few months.

"Please do not talk to her now," he asked.

In a grim and tense situation, two days passed. Arun, Prema, and Tara were getting all the documents together for the courier. On the third day, Arun thought the courier had come to pick up the documents, but to their surprise, the businessman came with Mia, Peter, Alisha, and the previous accountant.

"Against my will, my daughter, Alisha, forced me to reconsider," said the Businessman. "The previous accountant and Mia agreed after seeing the claims. Peter agreed with you on that day. So, I want to retract what I said, accusing you, Prema, the eye consultant, and Tax Authorities. My daughter convinced me that paying for your claims was better than losing millions of my business and possibly going to jail with my previous accountant. I have asked Alisha to issue cheques." He left the meeting with the old accountant and said, "Alisha manages the business now."

"Thank you for reconsidering and doing justice in the end," said Arun.

He called all the staff in reception to join. He asked Tara to type the invoices for writing the cheque for £25,000.

"Please, let me know how you would like to pay £103,000 to Ramesh and Neela. I prefer cash for the first payment followed by cheques or bank credit, as they do not have a bank account. £5,000 for Prema, please see my bank details to write the cheque."

Arun then asked Prema and her parents to come and meet the businessman's group. Alisha was happy to write the cheque and enquired why the same bank details. Prema said she was getting married to Arun on Wednesday, and they already had a joint account. Alisha congratulated them and wished them well. Arun wished Alisha good luck in the business. She said she was starting with a young team with Mia and Peter, hoping to have long innings. Alisha said that Tara was also in the same class but they rarely talked. She would pay six payments: £23,000 followed by five of £15,000 each. Arun agreed, and she paid cash for £23,000, which Tara collected and gave her a receipt for that.

Tara talked to Mia, as she was alone with Peter. Mentioning asking them both to work for Arun and her.

"Arun advised me to wait for a few months, and luckily you both were reinstated and working with Alisha."

Mia and Peter told Tara that they were not happy to work for Alisha as her dad's presence and control were strong, and they told her about quitting. Her dad seemed to favour that they both left, but Alisha was hesitant. In a day or so, she might accept their resignations.

"We would not say we are joining you."

They talked to Arun and left. Arun said he would decide on the monthly salary for Mia and Peter when they decided to join him. Tara said she would never discuss pay with anyone, even if they worked for her. Prema agreed it was good to follow for the next ten years! Arun suggested waiting for a couple of days for them to join. Within an hour, Mia and Peter came to see Tara, who took them to Arun and Prema.

"What happened?" asked Arun.

"We went to talk to Alisha," replied Mia, "but her dad shouted at us to get out forever. He did not want us to see Alisha. With tears, she bid us goodbye. She asked where we intended to seek work and we replied we did not know. So, we left to come here."

"We welcome you two to work here from tomorrow," said Arun. "We will meet after tea/coffee for an hour or so. Talk amongst yourself, but Mia and Peter, never say anything about your previous work or the people, as it is of no more interest to us. Let us enjoy the coffee and cakes."

They all met in the lounge. Liz was also there.

"All the youngsters should know that I have taken you all," said Arun, "and given you a good salary as I see your long-term potential to be very good. So far, each one of you has lived up to my expectations. I am happy to take Mia and Peter to our group. Mia will have a monthly salary of £600, and Peter at £500. Mia, as an accountant, will have a different focus from Tara, and they are unlikely to work together. Tara will be working on my work-related accounts, which will expand rapidly, and she will have assistants later. Mia, you will be the accountant for Tracy in her Stock Trading business. Also, you will guide Emma in managing her finance and be her financial guard. I will tell you what all you need to do, Mia. You will also have assistants later. Peter, you will be an understudy to me for a few months. I want Tracy to focus on Stock Trading only and let Mia advise on her financial status. Tracy is a specialist on two fronts. First, she should help her colleagues, including Prema, by buying shares in all top companies yielding good yearly dividends. They aim to have a regular income, for 30+ years, from these shares to supplement their pensions. Second, Tracy should focus on the investment front for others in the family, and she should also get outsiders to invest money through her. I believe her income potential is enormous and will impress the stockbroker community.

"I do not want any of you to think too big or that you are all indispensable. There is an experiment you all can do. Fill a bucket with water to an inch below the top. Take your cardigan off and remove the wristwatch if you are used to wearing it on the hand you dip in the water. Stir the water as fast and as long as you can. Then remove your hand and wait for a minute. The amount of cavity in the water is the measure of your indispensability. So, please wake up. No one is truly indispensable."

"Amazing experiment, Arun," said Grandpa. "I wish I had known this 30 years ago, to tell several big-headed medical doctors and put them in place."

"Thank you, Grandpa," said Arun. "All the youngsters need to focus on the work ahead of them. If you feel that you could do better working outside and want to leave me, please go ahead. But understand, once you leave me, my door is shut forever to you. It is not a threat but a promise. I will not be operating differently from tomorrow. I will attend cases in court as well.

"I have paid a deposit to a contractor building eight detached bedroomed houses, with all mod-cons, American style. I booked seven for all the staff here, Sally, Tara, Stella, Diana, Tracy, Mia, and Peter. Also, one house for Emma. Mia will have to ensure Emma and her two daughters are settled well in the house and local schools. Soon, you girls will get married, and have children and grandchildren, and I hope we all stay close until we retire. We should take good care of Emma and her children and take good care of each other. Until you all get married, let us have lunch and dinner here, and we all meet in the lounge after dinner for an update on all the information. If anyone has any questions or doubts, I will clarify. "

"Arun, all details are clearly explained, and there are no doubts," replied Tara.

"Let us all go for dinner," said Arun.

The following day at 9, Mrs. Dorothy and Mr. Dennis Compton came to find Tara and Stella at work. Diana took her grandparents to meet Arun and Prema. The Compton's wanted the three granddaughters to hear the good news.

"Arun, your letter did the trick," said Dennis. "My friend sincerely apologized as I mentioned his misbehaviour. But unfortunately for him and fortunately for us, his wife acted as secretary that day, and she thrashed him verbally. The result was she gave a peace offering of £2,500 in cash to each of the girls and boxes of chocolates. So, I thought it was mine and their lucky day. So, I went to see Diana's boss, a friend of

Tara's boss, and after the two bosses talked, he also gave £2,500 to Diana in cash."

The grandchildren hugged their grans and thanked Arun for his letter.

The following day at 7 am, Arun was in the office with Prema, with only three days to go to the wedding.

"How are you and your parents feeling about the wedding day, nervous, very happy, or mixed feelings?" he asked.

"I would say mixed but will change to all happy tears on the day," replied Prema. "All arrangements are satisfactory and no hassle from any issues."

"Do you think we should have no appointments booked for a week?" he asked.

"You said we should never stop Goddess Lakshmi from coming our way! So, we book appointments except for three days next week."

A call came, and Prema answered it.

"Good morning, I am Patrick Murphy, and I live in Finchley, London. I am contacting you on the advice of our local councils as you were outstanding in looking at all legal aspects at a low cost. I have a dispute with my neighbour on boundary issues. Is it possible for us to come by at ten today? I called two days ago and spoke to an old lady."

"Please come at ten this morning as agreed," said Arun.

Prema said that grandma had forgotten to enter the call. Arun wanted two hours to look at his old cases, and Prema agreed to join him at 9.30. At ten, a family of three saw all staff at the reception, and Diana, after the preliminary courtesies, took them to the meeting room and introduced Arun and Prema. She also told them about putting the recorder tape machine on. Within a few minutes, another family of three came, and Diana brought them to the meeting room.

"We are happy to see you all," said Arun, "but wish it was under more social circumstances. Patrick, please introduce the family and the issue for this meeting today."

"Aoife is my wife, and Daniel is my son. We have been living in the house for over 25 years, and we never had any issues with our neighbour. However, Trevor and his family moved in a year ago, and we have various problems."

"I will give both families some notes to discuss today's issues. Please read appendix 1 carefully."

He gave them 30 minutes to read and make notes.

"Before I request Trevor and Patrick, please list those causing concern to your family."

"Mainly, 5 and 6," said Patrick.

"5 Noise. A common complaint raised by people is to do with noise. 6 Trees and hedges. Overhanging trees are another common reason for neighbour disputes."

"Young Tom is a lovely lad but has frequent parties, and the music blares. When we complain, he turns the volume down, but it goes up after a short while. Sadly, the parties go till two or three a.m. Also, the overhanging tree from our side to their garden is the central issue."

"I would ask Trevor for his comments."

"Our primary concern was the tree spreading all over our gardens," said Trevor. "We would like it cut down, as it was dying. Both our old parents live locally, and we spend most of the weekends with them. Our son then had parties and playing music loudly. We accept Patrick's and other neighbours' complaints. We find it difficult to control a rebellious teenager."

"Please let me know the central aspect of your neighbourhood issue leading to this case?" asked Arun.

"I am against cutting down the 100-year-old tree," said Patrick. "I did not see any other issue."

"We see the tree is the root cause of our dispute since we moved to this house," said Trevor.

Arun said he wanted to ensure if any of these pertain to their grievances in the past. Patrick and Trevor confirmed that there were only issues they discussed earlier. Arun said that with their agreement, he would terminate the Free mediation and counseling and start his advice and consultancy for which fees were chargeable. The issues were more complicated than in their case, and his charge was £12,000. Once they agreed to what he said, he would proceed after a short coffee break. Patrick and Trevor decided on the next stage.

After the coffee break, they assembled in the meeting room with the audiotape on for recording.

"I need to contact a lawyer, tree surgeon, council, etc to get facts and charges for this case," said Arun. "Appendix 1 states the procedures and Appendix 2 the details of cost."

They re-joined after three days at 10 am after all the usual preliminaries.

"My decision for both the family considerations is in Appendix 2," said Arun. "The lawyer has studied the deeds and concluded that Patrick's family had let their garden encroach on Trevor's garden over the years. If reported to the council, they would levy a punitive penalty of £15,000, of which £10,000 was payable to Trevor. A balance of £5,000 council panel would keep and issue a warning to Patrick to rectify within two years. Failure to do so would mean a further penalty of £20,000, of which £15,000 is payable to Trevor, the balance to the council."

Arun said an experienced gardener could correct the encroachment within six months, for a fee of £6,000, which Trevor had to pay. The tree surgeon found the large tree was rotting in several places, and its deep roots had not spread to both buildings. He obtained permission from the council to remove the tree, and they agreed. He would complete the task in two months.

The council levied a fine of £7,500 on Trevor for his son violating the noise and peace of the neighbours.

"I agree to the charges," said Patrick, "and I will pay my part."

Patrick paid £22,500 to Tara towards his contribution.

"I refuse to accept the decision," said Trevor, "as I am paying more. I would contest it in court. I contest all payments; all are crooks, including you."

Trevor's wife and son felt that they had to pay their share and taking it to court would cost three to four times the amount stated here. A bitter family argument ensued. Following that, Trevor apologized for his rude remarks and paid £36,000 to Tara for various contributions. Tara made the payments and gave receipts to Patrick and Trevor.

Both families then left after thanking Arun, Tara, and others. Arun and Prema heaved a sigh of relief.

Arun said that with only a couple of days left, they should focus on the preparations for the wedding. Prema and Tara invited all the guests to come on time as the church doors would be closed promptly, and they should not miss the wedding. They got married in 30 min and had the registration certificates within an hour. The wedding lunch finished within two hours, and they all returned home by 5 pm.

Arun said they had to meet at 10 a.m. for a frank discussion the next day, and all should be free to express their opinions without fear of repercussions. All members of both the families of Arun and Prema, the six members of his staff, Emma, and the four grandparents were present.

"We all are attending here," said Arun, "and I, due to my prudish nature, prevented the youngsters from finding their boyfriends at an appropriate age. I will not put any restrictions on it from now. Your parents or grandparents may recommend anyone, and please decide what to do regarding friendship or marriage."

"Arun and Prema, Peter and I are in love and would like to get married asap. We would keep you all updated," said Mia.

All were pleased. The grans wanted their granddaughters to seek boyfriends soon and get married!

Appendix 1

These are only useful for the contesting parties in their disputes.

I have listed the typical issues involved, and please, indicate whether some or all applied to your case.

1. Lot line disputes.

2. Fence, landscaping, and outbuilding disputes.

3. Access disputes.

4. Adverse possession claims.

Common neighbour disputes

5. Noise. A common complaint raised by people is to do with noise.

6. Trees and hedges. Overhanging trees are another common reason for neighbour disputes.

7. Boundaries, fences, and driveways.

8. Shared amenities.

9. Party walls.

10. Abusive, anti-social, or violent issues.

11. Overhanging gutters.

"There are also other rules to observe," said Arun. "The Seven-Year Rule; so, for example, if you complain to the local planning authority about your neighbour doing something on their land that you don't like, but if they've been doing it for seven years or more, you might not have any luck stopping it.

"Who is a bad neighbour? A lousy neighbour is anyone who lives next door (or next floor) and gets on your nerves regularly by doing something that's not particularly illegal but exceptionally annoying. If it becomes uncomfortable for you to stay at home, it's a bad neighbour to blame.

"Lifestyle/environmental issues. Children or teenagers' behaviour. Dogs and other animals. Invasion of privacy.

"Your solicitor will consider the available evidence and, in particular:

- Deeds to your property along with that of your neighbour; and what they say about ownership of the land in dispute.
- previous sale agreements for both properties and any plans for your respective homes and gardens that may be attached.
- old photographs in which the location of previous fences, hedges, or even ditches separating your properties, and against which they can compare the area of current boundary features to see if any movement had taken place.
- Paperwork suggesting that the strip of land in dispute may have been sold off by a previous owner of your property so that it can no longer be said to be yours; and
- Any evidence produced by your neighbour suggests that they have been in occupation of the disputed land for 12 years or more without objection, which may now entitle them to claim ownership under the law of adverse possession."

Appendix 2

"I like to have the deeds of both the properties and three days to get comments from a lawyer," said Arun. "I will also get a good tree surgeon to comment on its status. The lawyer fee would be £10,000. The tree surgeon would charge £3,000 for his assessment and a further £5,000 for trimming. Let us meet after three days for my Consultancy chargeable service."

1. My charge is £12,000
2. The lawyer fee is £10,000
3. The tree surgeon fee is £8,000

Taking all these into consideration,

a. £36,000 (12,000+10,000+8,000+6,000) to be shared equally between Trevor and Patrick.
b. £15,000 penalty to Trevor
c. £7,500 penalty to Patrick.

If they were agreeable, Arun wanted to proceed with payment to the different parties and wanted Trevor and Patrick to give the account details to Tara, who would take appropriate action.

He agreed to pay £5,000 to the lawyer, £4,000 to the tree surgeon, £6,000 to Arun, £10,000 to Patrick, £5,000 to the council, and £6,000 to the gardener. He gave the bank details to Tara for the relevant transfers.

5

Systematic Approach for Long-Term Stability

Arun stated he would like all to assemble after breakfast for his plans. They all met in the lounge.

"I have decided to go to the courts to attend my cases," said Arun. "I had to contact the lawyers and hope to get invited for cases in 8-10 days. As I have previous experience in court cases, I would usually be an assistant to a senior lawyer handling the case. All my cases would involve going to local courts only. Local courts are where **all criminal matters** are first heard. From the most trivial breach right through to murder cases, they all start in Local Courts. In a matter where an accused is pleading not guilty to charges, there is a process where evidence is brought forward, and the guilt of the accused is decided. It usually takes 2 -3 weeks for simple cases to 10-12 weeks for complex cases. The senior lawyer may charge for simple cases, typically £30,000 per day, excluding court and associated costs, like other legal fees. Assistants earn 25% of senior lawyers per day. For complex cases, it would be £60,000 per day and the duration may be up to 12 weeks. For cases involving criminal matters, his fees may escalate to £100,000 per day and it may last 18-24 weeks.

"So, my income might vary from £7,500 to £25,000 per day depending on the type of case. Usually, it would be for four hours per day split over as two-hour duration; 10 to 12 noon and 2 to 4 pm in courts.

"I am depending on Prema and Diana to get cases for me to deal with from 7 to 9 am and 5 to 7 pm. I also rely on Tara to manage all the financial issues. I intend to work on Saturdays and would hope to have 2 cases only if the clients need to see me on Saturdays. Otherwise, it would be a rest day.

"Typically, my fees would be £1,000 per hour. I estimate an average income of £4,000 per day, in addition to an income of £7,500 from the court cases. I might increase my fees for home cases depending on the specialty of the case and the wealth of the clients contesting.

"Mia will play a crucial role in my plans to sort out details for HMRC for the bonus and other payments. I intend to pay immediately:

1. a bonus of £5,000 every quarter to the 5 staff – Diana, Tara, Stella, Mia, and Peter. Sadly, Tracy is not included as she operates as an independent businesswoman and not working for me. 5,000 x 5 = £25,000. £100,000 yearly

2. £200 quarterly bonus to all service staff – in the kitchen, garden, drivers, security, cleaners, etc. No one is to be excluded. 200 x10 = 2,000 est. £8,000 yearly

3. £1,000 on the birthdays of all in our small community including Tracy, Emma, and her two daughters. 16 x £1,000 = £16,000 yearly. £300 for 10 service staff = 3,000 yearly.

4. Increase of Salary to all staff (5) in 6 months by £1,000 each. £5,000 this year.

5. Total outlay £132,000 per year (/12 months /22 days per month = £500 per day)

"Any points to raise, please let me know?"

"We are impressed with your earning potential and the range of cases you might be handling," said Liz. "Also, the bonus to office staff, service staff, birthday gifts, and salary increases to key staff are commendable."

"My income would cover all increases," said Arun, "and I want to have a well-knit group committed to staying with us even after their retirement.

"On behalf of all we thank you," said Tracy, "and would never leave this group even after marriage. Mia is already sorted with Peter. I will try to find a husband who would also work for you, Arun."

"We hope your plan works out, Tracy," he replied. "Now the meeting is over, and we all should focus on our respective tasks after tea/coffee, and snacks."

They all met at lunchtime and Diana said she had two cases for the next day.

"Diana, I am very delighted," said Arun, "and need to know the details to prepare for tomorrow. I contacted my mentor stating I would be involved in court cases during weekdays and wanted his help as he knew several senior lawyers. I promised to pay £2,500 for his introduction and offer for each case. He recommended Mr. Tyson, who lives only 5 mins from our house, and that he was a very senior lawyer needing an assistant. He told about me Mr. Tyson who wanted me to start on Monday. I spoke to Mr. Tyson, who welcomed me and wanted me to start at 9.45 am in the county court. It was a highly criminal felony case and the first two days would be procedural and I should get a feel for the case. Mr. Tyson was the defence attorney, even though he would have preferred to be the prosecution attorney. He has a case report with some details and I will collect it later today and be prepared when I see him. Diana, please tell me about the two cases?"

"The first client was a lady, middle-aged, very wealthy. She has a disagreement with another rich lady of similar age about a young girl. They both claim her as their lesbian partner. She agreed to come at 7 am on Monday. The second is the LGBT case, here two 50+ ladies claiming a toyboy. They agreed to come at 5 pm Monday."

"Most interesting," said Arun, "and thank you, Diane. I will send the chauffeur to collect the report from Mr. Tyson and will be in my room reading about the cases. I will see you all during dinner."

As Arun wanted his dinner sent upstairs, all the others missed him and Liz wished him all the best in his endeavours.

At 6.45 am all assembled at the reception with Arun and Prema in the main interview room. Sheila brought their coffee which they finished quickly and were ready in 5 minutes. At 7 am, three ladies came, 2 were over 50 years and the other third one was 20 years. They were brought by Diane, who introduced Arun and Prema and switched the tape recorder on. Arun asked them to introduce themselves.

"I'm Sylvia Robson. I live in South Kensington, London. I am 51 years and my dad owns diamond mines in South Africa. He has a lot of jewelry shops in the UK. I am his only daughter. I have known Miss Mary Stuart for a few months and we have a lesbian relationship. I will continue later."

"I'd like to stop here," said Arun, "and will ask Prema, my assistant, to take Miss Stuart to the next office to be with Diana. She will not know what we discuss here. Is that ok with you, Mary?"

"I'd prefer to leave the other room before the other lady introduces herself," replied Mary.

Arun asked the lady for details.

"I'm Penelope Jones. I am 55 years old and live in Chelsea, London. My dad owns a lot of properties in Rwanda worth over £100 million. I am the only daughter and my younger brother and his family in Rwanda look after our properties. My dad told me that he would give a maximum £20M, due to my lesbian relationships and the rest to my brother. I would also get £120,000 per year on interest too. I have known Mary for 6 months only and it appears longer than she knew Sylvia."

"My charge for this case is £30,000 split equally between you two," said Arun. "My first hour or part thereof is FREE. After that, it will be charged as I mentioned above. If you both agree then I will proceed."

Both Sylvia and Penelope agreed.

"I want each of you to let me know where and how you met Mary and what was your relationship with Mary?" he asked them.

"I met Mary in a social meeting at a school function," said Penelope, "and I approached her directly for a dinner meeting that evening. I gave her £50, my address, and asked her to come by Taxi at 6 pm. I saw her arrive on time and made her sit next to me on the sofa. I then put my arm around her and kissed her. She was very willing and did not raise any objections. I told her that she was my exclusive companion and then I would pay her £30,000 per year. She said she needed time to think about it. I also offered £500 for each visit and she smilingly accepted."

"I met Mary at a village fair," said Sylvia, "and she was with a few of her friends. I befriended her and she told me of her lesbian affairs for over 10 years. She was extremely friendly and stayed the night. I offered her £25,000 per year and £400 per visit and she said she needed time and would let me know soon."

"Did Mary respond and what did she say?" asked Arun.

"Two days ago, she declined," replied Penelope. "She complimented me on my generosity and soft manners but she was young and would stay with her age group lest she missed the fun. She returned the £500 which I refused. She said she was sad to reject two good offers."

"She said similar things two days ago," said Sylvia, "and returned the £400 which I refused."

"Then where is the case and on what basis are you fighting?" asked Arun.

"I felt that without Sylvia, I could have had Mary for a long relationship," replied Penelope.

"I felt the same about Penelope," said Sylvia.

"My Free Consultation is finished," said Arun. "I will talk to Mary and give my pronouncements which will incur the charge of £30,000 total. In a court, you both would have spent 5 to 6 times this amount. If you both agree, I will see Mary."

They both agreed.

Arun went to the next room and asked Mary to speak frankly to him to decide on this case once and for all, with no comeback situation for the three. She agreed.

"Mary, why did you go for dinner? Were you expecting a new relationship?"

"I made a mistake. Went for kicks and fell for the sweet talk of the mature ladies. Their money also tempted me."

"Did you favour one over the other as your answer left that doubt in their minds?"

"I am not articulate and did not think of the implications. I did not favour one against the other. I wanted to go back to my age group. I had learned a lesson and will keep my distance from older people."

"Be careful and please do not make such stupid mistakes from now on. Let us meet them in the other room. You should return their money too."

Arun said he had talked to Mary and there was a colossal mistake by the youngster. She did not favour anyone. As she is not articulate, she did not realise the implications put on her comments.

"My final comments are as follows: this case should not have risen between two mature and wealthy people; Mary made a colossal mistake and did not favour one against the other; she was not articulate and did not realise the implications of her comments. She is prepared to return the money to you both for the valuable lessons learned. As there is no case, my charges will not apply. I leave you two to decide whether to pay me for my time spent."

"We are in full admiration of you, Arun," said Penelope, "in admitting this as no real case to put a handling fee. I did not want Mary to return £500 and wish her all the best for the future. I will pay £6,000 to you to compensate you for your valuable time. Thank you, Arun, Mary, Prema, and others."

"I echo Penelope's feelings wholeheartedly," said Sylvia, "and I do not need £400 from Mary. I will also pay £6,000 to you for your time, Arun. You are a wonderful gentleman, and I'm delighted you have a keen young team and your family of 3 medics involved. I would preach about your laurels to others."

"Thank you, Penelope and Sylvia, for your generosity, and Mary for coming to attend this case."

The visitors left and Prema gave the two cheques to Tara to process in due course.

Arun went to the court by 9.45 am to meet Mr. Tyson. After the day's court proceedings, he returned home by 4.30 pm.

Arun wanted Diana to bring the clients to the interview room. Diane then brought the three people to the interview room, introduced Arun and Prema, and turned the tape recorder on for recording all conversations and getting their approval. Arun asked them to introduce themselves and state the reasons for the case. He wanted the young man to leave with Prema to the other room where Diana was going to be with him. Prema returned to be with Arun.

"I usually offer Free consultation for an hour and after that, my charges would be £40,000 to be shared equally. The young man would not have to pay anything. If you both agree, we can proceed."

They both agreed.

"I am Samantha Hardwick. I am 45 years old and more interested in sex. Please call me Sam. My parents do not approve of this and they do not speak to me. However, my dad is mega-rich due to working in Middle Eastern oil exploration and my mum hails from affluent parents. I was given £25 M and I live in Oxford in an upmarket property in the university complex. I have an annual income from shares of £120,000. I liked Keith Hamilton of 24 years; a well-built muscular lad and he has been my toy-boy for over 2 years."

"Sam," said Arun, "I will come back to you after the other client speaks."

"I am Jackie Rance. I am 51 years old and interested in sex. I had several Toy Boys over the years and Keith was the latest for over 1 year. He mentioned being a Toy Boy for me only and only then I knew about Sam."

"Sam has Keith mentioned his preference to Jackie?" asked Arun.

"Not so far."

"How much did you pay him for his services?"

"I pay £300 for each visit and £20,000 yearly as a retainer. He comes 3 times a week."

"Jackie, how well off are you?" asked Arun, "and how much did you pay Keith for his services?"

"My husband works in the oil industry and his wealth is over £30 M. He had adulterous relationships for years and as a divorce settlement, I got £10M. I get £60,000 per year on my investments. I pay £400 for each visit and £30,000 yearly as a retainer. He comes 4 times a week."

"In such lesbian and Toy Boy relationships it is the accepted norm that the age difference should not exceed 10 years," said Arun. "Sam, in your case it is 21 years and Jackie, in your case it is 27 years. There is a formula used at times – your age divided by 2 and add 7 years as the age for lesbian relationships. Sam, in your case the maximum age of the person should be 29.5 years. Jackie in your case it should be 32.5 years. I think you both will have to evaluate this factor for future lasting relationships. I will talk to Keith privately and then we all will meet to take a decision."

Arun and Prema went to the next room and the tape recorder was put on. Diane came to stay with Sam and Jackie.

"I heard from Sam and Jackie," said Arun, "about your visits to them and the retainer payments from each of them. Jackie also told me that you preferred a relationship only with her. Please let me know your comments which will be confidential. I am envious of your stamina but it is not the subject of our discussions."

"In life," said Keith, "I was blessed with my personality and adequate equipment which pleased both the ladies. Initially, I was a freelancer and was happy but no retainers. Despite the age difference, Jackie had more stamina to match and paid me well. I preferred her. I felt embarrassed to tell Sam and was waiting for an opportunity to mention it. These two moneyed ladies were keen on making a case to fight it out. They said your costs would be a lot cheaper than going to court."

"Keith, thanks for your frank comments, and let us move to join the other two for my decisions."

They all moved to join Sam and Jackie.

"I had a frank talk with Keith," said Arun, "and I feel I can give my decisions. It is chargeable from now for £40,000 and if you both agree, I will proceed with my deliberations."

They both agreed.

"I talked to Keith and he enjoyed both your companies; however, he preferred to be with Jackie. He wanted to find a suitable time to tell you but you both proceeded with a case that was going out of his control. Sam, under the circumstances would you be prepared to let him go to Jackie from now on?"

"If he has stated his preference, I do not want him from now on. I feel insulted and I could look elsewhere for my enjoyment and comfort. I will not pay any more retainer fees to Keith."

"I am delighted that Keith will service me full-time," said Jackie. "We are sorry for not discussing calmly the issues involved and coming to an amicable solution. Arun, you saved us a lot of money by not taking it to court."

"I am glad you are both happy and for me, it was a case that had a solution staring at me. If you both feel you should reduce the payment to me, please do so. I leave it to your decisions."

"I will pay £20,000 of my share happily," said Jackie and wrote a cheque as requested by Prema and she gave it to Tara. She thanked Arun, and all the staff and left with Keith.

"I will also pay my share of £20,000," said Sam, "but I am sad I lost Keith forever." She also gave a cheque to Diana, thanked Arun, and all the staff, and left.

Prema asked Tara to credit the cheques and Mia to deal with HMRC issues. They all went to their respective rooms and agreed to meet for dinner soon.

They all had a nice dinner and met in the lounge for the usual updates.

Grans and Liz told Arun that they were astonished he had earned £52,000 within 4 hours from the two cases at home.

"When two wealthy ladies fight on a lesbian issue over a youngster," said Arun, "money is not their focus, it's the youngster. It was ripe ground to charge a high fee and I succeeded. Even asking them to pay what they wished after the first case I knew they would speak highly of my attitude as being fair and not money-grabbing. Those two will bring more clients to me. My court case was a routine procedure and it will continue for another 2 days. My income for the day is £7,500 only. I am quite happy. I am tired and will speak with Diana and Prema about tomorrow's two cases."

The three left for the office.

"The case in the morning," said Diana, "involves three men entering the property at night and attacking the owner, an Indian, a post office, and a small shop owner, who had to be hospitalised. Cash worth £800 was stolen and two gold necklaces worth a total of £2,500 were also stolen. The Indian owner is suing for the return of the missing items and compensation for loss of earnings etc. They will come at 7 am.

"The evening case is more complicated in that it involves not paying returns on investments amounting to fraud. It also concerns tax crimes. The parties agreed to come 15 minutes early for the 5 Pm case hearing."

Arun thanked Diana and retired to sleep.

The next morning, Arun with Prema entered the main Interview room and Diana brought the clients. She introduced Arun and Prema and put the tape recorder on after telling the clients. She then left for the reception.

Arun asked the clients to introduce themselves and outline the case. He said the first hour of Consultation and counseling was FREE but his fee for the complex case is £2,400 payable by the person bringing the case and £600 payable by the loser. The clients accepted the terms.

"I am Mr. Shyam Patel, the owner of a post office with a small shop. I live with my wife and two daughters, 16 and 12, in the flat above. I heard a noise at 12 midnight and the front door glass was broken. I asked my wife to call the police using the phone in the bedroom. In the commotion, my daughters got up but my wife asked them to close their bedroom door and put a table behind it to prevent the robbers from breaking in. She also closed our bedroom door. I went downstairs and three white men aged below 30 years with rods and one wielding a gun hit me and demanded money, saying refusal to pay would mean my wife and daughters would be raped. I was forced to open the safe and they took £800 and the two necklaces my wife kept for safekeeping. Hearing the noise of the police car, they rushed out. The police came and took my statement. They went upstairs and my wife and daughters opened their doors and told the events from midnight. The girls were shivering as this was the first time a robbery with violence had taken place. Because of speakers in the bedrooms, they could hear all the conversations clearly compounding the girls' fear for their dad and the family. There was a tape recording of all conversations. The police took all the statements and gave us a copy for records. They also took the tape to the police lab for voice recognition to catch the culprits. Within an hour they reported catching the three men and confiscated £800 and the jewels. The next day we identified the jewels as ours as we had taken a photograph of these two items."

"Most interesting," said Arun, "and I will come back to you a little later after hearing about the other client."

"I am Mr. John English and I represent us including two of my friends. We told the police it was a mistaken identity. That night we met three other friends who told us to take a bag that they would collect in a few days. They drove off in a car. We were walking and were caught by the police. They confiscated the bag and found £800 cash and two jewels. We refused to identify our friends and their car. We were released on bail. We three are unemployed and rarely do we go for assault or rape. Small burglaries we do like snatching handbags etc. when people are careless. We have nothing to do with this case. We must appear in court in two weeks and report to the police each day. I have nothing more to add."

"Mr. Patel," said Arun, "as owning a post office, you could have the case and costs covered by the Post Office. Why did you want to waste money by coming to me?"

"Usually, Post-Office cases take a long time before it goes to court and we heard about your Counselling and the low costs charged by you. People praised you and I would have to pay 10% to the Post Office of their total cost. I wanted a resolution quickly."

"I decided to reduce my fees to £1,200 for Mr. Patel and £300 for John and his two friends," said Arun. "If it is acceptable, the FREE session is over and I will proceed with my judgment. Is it acceptable to both parties?"

Both agreed immediately.

"Mr. Patel has a cast iron case," said Arun. "If he reconciles with the affected party, Post Office may compensate for his injuries and loss of earnings as they do not have to incur high costs. His tapes of conversations would mean a certain conviction to John and his friends. The Police lab would ask the three to speak and compare with the tape from Mr. Patel. Property crimes would be soon established. The intention of sex crimes, despite no sex being involved, would also be established when the case comes to court in two weeks. John and his friends would lose in the civil court. They could be fined and given a custodial sentence. However, as they inflicted bodily wounds on Mr. Patel, this could be classed as a Felony and could be decided as in sections D or E. This would mean a prison sentence and a fine. My advice to John and his friends is to admit the guilt now before the case comes to court so that they may have a lighter sentence. I also feel that you three pay a notional £600 for injuries caused to Mr. Patel. The Post Office would compensate for his loss of earnings. I have finished my judgment of the case. I await your comments and payment by cheque to Prema."

"I am very pleased about your judgments," replied Mr. Patel, "and hope the Post Office compensates me. I will issue a cheque for £1,200 to Prema and many thanks for reducing your fee. I agree to the notional payment for injuries caused by the intruders."

"We also agree with you, Mr. Arun," said John, "and admit guilt tomorrow when we go to the police station. We will pay cash to Prema and pay cash to Mr. Patel."

Arun advised John to get signed receipts from Prema and Mr. Patel. Both the parties left after all the formalities and thanked Arun, Prema, Diana, Arun's grans, and all staff.

Arun and Prema left the interview room and Arun got ready to go to court. Arun went to the court to meet Mr. Tyson. After the day's court proceedings, he returned home by 4.30 pm.

Diana brought the two clients and introduced Arun and Prema, switched on the tape recorder, and left.

"Please introduce yourselves before we proceed," asked Arun.

"I am Mr. Soloman Knight, a private investor using the private company of Mr. Tom Smith."

"I am Mr. Tom Smith, the M.D. of a large £20 M investment company, and helping Soloman with his investment for over 5 years. He has brought this case claiming compensation."

"I will get the details from each one of you. I offer FREE consultation and conciliation for one hour and after that my charges would be £40,000, £30,000 payable by Tom, and £10,000 payable by Soloman. If agreeable we will proceed."

"We had good references from a few people," said Tom, "on how you help to reduce the huge costs involved in going to court. I agree to the fees."

"I had good comments about you too, Arun, and agree to the fees," said Solomon.

"Soloman, please let me know your side of the case before I turn to Tom," asked Arun.

"I have been trading with Tom's company for over 5 years and was extremely happy with their performances. My investments grew by 80% in that period. I usually invest £10,000 with a proviso not to exceed £50,000. If my losses were to exceed that they should not take money from my account to which they have access. In my last transaction, they had withdrawn £120,000 from my account. It was a shock to me and I am claiming compensation for the return of £70,000 over the limit set and some penalty payment of £25,000."

"Have you ever invested exceeding the limit without notifying them?" asked Arun.

"Never, as I strictly control the trading to the limits agreed with them."

"Thank you, Soloman. Let me request Tom to present his case."

"I am giving some documents to your assistant, Prema and give you 10 minutes to study that," replied Tom.

Arun and Prema read the documents and Arun was prepared to listen to Tom.

"Soloman was one of the model clients," said Tom. "Unfortunately, three times in the last 5 years he exceeded his limit and we invested and on all three occasions, he gained 10-20%. We told him verbally and in writing about his exceeding the limit but we traded and he benefitted. He replied stating it would never happen again. We told him to increase the upper limit which he was not agreeable to. He exceeded the second time and to our request, he refused but only apologised. We told him in writing that if it happened again, we would recover our money from his account and inform him. This time his investment made a gain of 15% and we told him about exceeding the limit and he did not reply. Then the stocks nearly crashed and he incurred a loss of £75,000 and we took £70,000 from his account to compensate us. Solomon's comment about not exceeding the limit in the last five years was incorrect."

"Soloman, these papers are proof of your not telling us the truth. Please clarify," said Arun.

"I forgot these incidents," said Solomon, "and I could see my failings. I am a small personal investor and losing £70,000 from one's account was a big loss and shock to me."

"Many security firms, even when they are wrong, settle early for a very small percentage," said Arun, "often less than 5%, on investors' loss. Here Tom has genuine grounds to recover his money due to your mismanagement. You still owe him £5,000. I will say the FREE consultancy period is over and I will start my judgment with a fee to be paid of £30,000 by Tom and £10,000 by Solomon. May I proceed with my judgment, please?"

Tom agreed immediately but Solomon only agreed after a long pause.

"My judgment is straightforward as the case and events lend themselves a solution. Tom was entitled to recover his money but he was still owed £5,000. Solomon has no grounds for any compensation as he let his losses build up despite being alerted by Tom. My solution is to apply the 5% rule, which for £75,000 would amount to £3,750. Tom may agree to forfeit £3,750 or as a gesture the whole balance of £5,000. As regards my fee, I leave it to you both to decide what to pay me for my time on this unique and sad case. My advice to you Solomon is please watch your money like a hawk and do not lose focus due to other issues."

"I am very impressed with your solution," said Tom, "and as I have not lost out, I will pay the full amount of £30,000. I will waive Solomon's payment of £5,000." He issued a cheque to Prema after getting the details and she gave it to Diana.

"I realise my mistake," said Solomon, "and I apologise to both of you for my behaviour. I have great respect for Tom and his dealings. I will deal with his company only and try to recover the losses through gains in the future. Arun, I will pay your fee of £10,000, and thanks for suggesting not having to pay £5,000 to Tom. I thank Tom for waiving the amount."

He issued a cheque to Prema for £10,000 for Arun. They both shook hands and thanked Arun, Prema, and the team before leaving.

Arun and the team went for dinner. After the dinner discussion, Arun explained the two cases in detail to all. Liz appreciated earning £41,500 that day and admired his skill of charging as per the client's wealth. Tara confirmed, depositing the cheques and Mia assured her about dealing with HMRC issues. She said all in the team and staff were paid their salary rises and quarterly bonuses and dealt with all HMRC issues. Grans appreciated Arun's income potential and how it was escalating.

Arun wanted to retire after spending a few minutes with Diana and Prema about the next day's two cases.

"No one wanted to come tomorrow, thinking you were on honeymoon," said Diana. "We did not push them to. So please take the next few days as a period of well-earned rest."

On that note, Arun, Prema, and all retired to bed.

The next morning, Arun had a message that there was no need to go to the courts till the following Monday. All were happy about the unexpected rest and the girls were planning a picnic. In an hour all went to a nearby park with a small lake and started enjoying the samosas etc.

"I want to say something of interest to all of us including Emma and Tracy," said Arun. "I want to start a new company 'Arun Legal Co-op Enterprises Limited'. The salient points are all staff including service staff as a group, making 13 members, would become 4% shareholders and enjoy sharing of profits each year. All details are covered in Appendix 2."

Liz and Grans admired Arun's bold approach in forming a cooperative venture for legal business, hitherto, never ventured anywhere in the world, to their best knowledge. All started singing, "He's a jolly good fellow" and ended the picnic on a wonderful note.

The talk after dinner was in total praise of Arun and how the scenario would change once Mia dealt with the HMRC procedures for Coop. Arun, Prema, her parents, Liz, and Grans left for their rooms but the other girls with Emma had a nice natter about their fortunes.

The next day was a free day and Arun was enjoying his coffee in the breakfast room with Prema, Liz, grans, and all the staff. There was a call that Diana answered. It was a long call and she told Arun it was a family feud regarding money allocation between a brother and his sister. They wanted to come in an hour and it was agreed.

All the staff were in the reception and Liz with grans was also there. The first set of clients included two members and the second set included two members. They were introduced to Arun and Prema and the tape recorder was put on after notifying them.

"Please introduce yourselves first and briefly state your case," asked Arun.

"I'm Mr. Jeff Jones. I used to live in Australia as I was born there but I had a quarrel with my dad when I was courting Jennifer and after an acrimonious fight left Sydney to come to the UK. Jennifer's dad was from Swansea, Wales but he returned to the UK a few months before we came to London. As a marketing professional for a chemical company, I got a good job in London. Jennifer was a senior receptionist in a GP's surgery in Sydney and she got a similar position in a large GP practice. We live in Chelsea. I had to give a lot of background before I could talk about the case. Would it be, ok?"

"It is very interesting," replied Arun, "and let us get both your backgrounds and we have lunch here, purely vegetarian only. Once the details are known, my Free mediation and counseling will start. If that is acceptable, we will proceed."

Both parties were happy with the arrangement.

"I am the eldest son," said Jeff, "and my sister was Sylvia. My case involves her but we will address the details later. Because of my toxic relations with my dad, I changed my surname to Jones, Jennifer's surname. My dad was born in the UK and worked only in Chester before emigrating to Sydney, Australia. He married my mother and we were born in the 3rd and 5th years after their marriage. My parents emigrated before we were born. My dad was a womaniser and he had sexual relationships with his patients and prostitutes. Due to several women complaining, he was struck off from practice. Sadly, he contracted the venereal disease and died five years ago. My mother divorced him when we were 12 and 10 years and we were brought up by her. Due to my dad forcing himself on her, she contracted the venereal disease and died a year later. He told my mum that all his wealth would go to her. But as she divorced him, she got only £50,000. He refused to pay her more even though he had wealth of £450,000 from his pensions, and stock market earnings. I understand his new Will stipulated all his money goes to my sister. So, I had none of his money. When my mum died, she did not have any Will. As she always wanted us to have equal shares, £25,000 came to me and £25,000 to my sister. The Lawyer in Sydney said there was no Will ever written by my dad. During the period he had the venereal disease, he made a joint account with my sister and when he died there was no legal requirement to split the money as it was in her account. Due to difficult circumstances here, I sought £150,000 from my sister but she refused. My case was to get a fair share."

"It is sad to hear your side of the story," said Arun. "Let me hear her side."

"I'm Mrs. Sylvia Timms. I agree with most of the comments made by my brother. However, he always had a short fuse and there was never a quiet conversation between my dad and Jeff. Each used to wind up the other. I was surprised Jeff stayed in the house and put up with my dad's caustic remarks even after he was working. However, when he was in love with Jennifer, my dad tried to seduce and misbehave with her. Only then Jeff emigrated to the UK. I hated my dad for his behaviour. Fortunately, I was in love with Robert, married him and we had a separate apartment. I used to visit my dad once a week and he wanted a joint bank account with me. He arranged it a year before he passed away. He was always bitter about Jeff and hated him. We emigrated to the UK after my mum died and we now live in South Kensington. Jeff never came to Sydney after my dad died and after my mum's death. He never bothered to talk to me for years and as we are in the UK, he wants money as if it is his birthright. Robert got transferred through Imperial Tobacco Company from Australia to the UK and had a senior management job in the head office in London. I used to do stock market trading in a small way having my own company but not set up in the UK yet. I have nothing to add now, maybe later."

As it was nearing lunchtime, Prema arranged lunch for the six of them in the kitchen adjacent to the interview room. After lunch, they met in the interview room.

"As we had discussed the preliminaries for two hours," said Arun, "do we need to continue further or shall I proceed with my judgment and my fees?"

They both wanted to proceed with his judgment.

"From now on, I will be charging for my discussions. My fee is £30,000 in total and each must pay £15,000. Australia, like the UK, has rigid rules like HMRC here about inheritance tax of 40% of the transfer of parental wealth over and above the allowance of £50,000. On that basis, Tax due to Australian inheritance would be 40% of £400,000 equal to £160,000. Transfer of money in a joint account would be deemed as inheriting the money and normal banking rules do not override inheritance tax rules. Fortunately, Sylvia, you emigrated here and, if no one creates trouble for you by informing the Australian tax office, you are safe for now.

"Your dad had never written a Will and dying intestate would mean an equal share for the children as the wife had divorced him. For your mother's small amount of £50,000, there would be no inheritance tax arising ever.

"My advice to you is to transfer £225,000 to Jeff as soon as conveniently possible. Should someone cause trouble then Jeff is also involved in not paying inheritance tax and pays the penalties as you would be doing? My second piece of advice is that each of you puts £80,000 in a savings account so that it is kept aside for any future claims. Please regard the £160,000 as not belonging to you both. If you both agree, then I will proceed to payment procedures."

"I never realised the inheritance tax complications," said Sylvia, "and I will transfer £225,000 to Jeff's account once I have his account details. I will also pay £15,000 towards your fee and thank you for such a friendly and family-type resolution on this case which unnecessarily caused a lot of friction between us."

"I am very grateful to you, Arun," said Jeff, "for a speedy and just resolution, considering tax implications. I will pay £25,000 in appreciation for your services. I will give my bank details to Sylvia now and I will issue a cheque for you once I have your account details."

"Prema will sort out the account and payment details," said Arun. "Sylvia and Jeff, let us go for Tea/coffee and discuss a suitable job for Sylvia. I would request you two to bury the hatchet and start a new life as an affectionate brother and sister and forget the past and your dad. Despite your inheritance, your dad had despicable behaviour in passing the venereal disease to your mum and in trying to seduce Jennifer. He was worth forgetting."

Without replying, Sylvia gave a huge hug to Jeff with tears rolling down their eyes. Prema gave the account details of Arun and to her surprise, Sylvia paid £25,000 as did Jeff.

"I will ask Mia to tell you four about our coop company," said Arun, "introduce all the staff and my mum and grans. I will ask Tracy to talk to you about working with her. She may be young but is very skilled and if you were not prepared to accept her as your senior, unfortunately, there is no job I could offer. Not that you came to me for a job offer but talking to you I felt we could have a long-term relationship."

"Jeff and I learned a lot of things today," said Sylvia, "and I would not seek a job outside when I could work for you with such a homely crowd. Let me talk to Tracy after our snack."

"Let Tracy and Mia talk to the four of you after tea," replied Arun. "Let us meet for dinner and discuss this during our usual meeting after dinner."

The two families had good exposure to the people and Arun's family and the Coop company formation with details. Sylvia knew only she could be a shareholder if she decided to work for Tracy. At the meeting, she said, "I have decided to work with and for Tracy, and I'd like to start from Monday if allowed."

"I usually deal with all employees except for Tracy," said Prema, "who has her own company."

"The formation of the Arun Coop Legal Enterprises Ltd, simplifies a lot of employment procedures which I would explain after you join on Monday," said Tracy.

"I would like the four of you to stay with us from Friday evening to Sunday evening and have food with us," said Prema and they agreed.

A few weeks went by and Mia set up the new Co-op company and Sylvia started enjoying her work. Arun's income was growing and his court commitments also increased.

Unfortunately, the story ends here. Goodbye to all!

Please read the two attachments below if interested, on procedures and financial details for the Coop:

Appendix 1

What is the difference between theft, robbery and burglary?

In reports about crimes where money or property are taken, "theft", "burglary" and "robbery" are terms often used interchangeably. There are, however, very clear differences between these offences.

Put very simply, someone is guilty of robbery if he steals from a person using force or makes them think force will be used. Theft means taking someone's property but does not involve the use of force. Burglary means illegally entering a property in order to steal property from it.

Below is a summary of each offence and what it involves.

Theft

In legislation "a person is guilty of theft if he dishonestly appropriates property belonging to another with the intention of permanently depriving the other of it." This could mean someone stealing from a shop, picking someone's pocket, stealing a bicycle or car, an employee stealing from their workplace or a guest stealing something from a house during a party.

The maximum sentence for theft is seven years.

Robbery

The definition as set out in legislation is as follows: "A person is guilty of robbery if he steals, and immediately before or at the time of doing so, and in order to do so, he uses force on any person or puts or seeks to put any person of being then and there subjected to force".

This can include a street mugging or robbery of a shop, business or security vehicle.

Due to the violent nature of robbery, it is treated as being more serious than theft and the maximum sentence is life.

Burglary

Burglary is committed when an offender either:

1. a) as a trespasser enters a building intending to steal, inflict grievous bodily harm or do unlawful damage; or,
2. b) having entered as a trespasser steals or attempts to steal, or inflicts or attempts to inflict grievous bodily harm.

There are three types of burglary recognised in law. These are:

Domestic burglary – Burglary of a dwelling

This type of burglary occurs when an offender enters, as per the definition above, a building in which people live. This generally refers to houses or flats. It also includes boats and vehicles in which people live, such as caravans, and can include domestic outhouses or garages if they are linked to a house.

The maximum sentence is 14 years.

Non-domestic burglary – Burglary of premises other than a dwelling – Theft Act 1968 (s9)

This type of burglary relates to buildings which are not lived in, such as shops or offices.

The maximum sentence is 10 years.

Burglary can be committed when a person is permitted to enter a home or other premises but then goes to a room or area where they are not permitted to be and steals something. For example, if a person steals items on display in a shop that would be theft, but if they go into a storeroom and steal something, that would be burglary.

Aggravated burglary

This offence is committed when, at the time of a burglary, the offender has with him any firearm or imitation firearm, any weapon of offence or any explosive.

Where a weapon is used to attack someone at the property in the course of the burglary the offender would also normally be charged with an assault offence, or alternatively, they could be charged with robbery.

The maximum sentence for aggravated burglary is life.

Appendix 2

"Before that, I want Mia to do some calculations. For my estimated earnings this year, how much tax would I have to pay to HMRC? Nothing is confidential now."

"Your estimated income is £1,200,000," replied Mia. "The yearly expenses after salaries, etc. is £1M. At 80% tax payable, it would amount to £800,000. A very hefty sum."

"I am intending to make all 12 present staff, including Tracy and Emma, shareholders and pay them a bonus of £40,000 each. I would also pay for all Service Staff Group (SSG) £40,000.

"Bonuses would total £480,000," said Mia. "All (13) would have to pay 20% tax which would amount to £96,000. Then the taxable income after expenses is £520,000 and tax at 80% is only £416,000. Net tax to HMRC is £512,000. A saving of £288,000. Wonderful plan Arun."

"Each of the 12 pays into a new company," said Arun, "which you had to set up Mia in a few days as Arun Legal Co-op Enterprises Ltd, in a Trust form and each of 13 contribute £40,000 for 4% share. I would pay the balance to make it £1M for a 48% share. All future legal bookings should be made through this company only."

"All shareholders would have to pay their own NI, Pensions etc," added Mia, "but entitled to buy a car or any vehicle and charge it to their individual expenses before paying tax. SSG would be paid their usual NI, Pensions and Tax as at present. SSG is entitled to the share of the profit."

"I would recommend all other staff and SSG to use Mia as their accountant and prepare the accounts for HMRC," said

Arun. "For this service, they should pay her an annual charge by mutual agreement."

"Thanks, Arun," said Mia, "for getting this extra business! I should say that if the company has a similar income of £2M and expenses including bonuses are say £700,000 the profit is £500,000. After-tax of 80%, £260,000 is after-tax profit. With 13 Partners, a dividend of £18,000 each would amount to £234,000. A balance of £26,000 is retained for future emergency expenses. The dividend next year would be equivalent to 45%. From next year, it would be a clean dividend of 100% as there would be no investment. However, once we become shareholders, we have to forgo overtime for late evening, weekend work, time in lieu etc.

"In the case of SSG, with present workers of 10, the individual dividend amount is £1,800. In case 5 workers join, the dividend of £18,000 would be divided by 15 amounting to £1,600. If a person leaves after 3 months of the next year, the person can take only a quarter of the dividend and the rest would be in the SWG Trust Fund. If the share of the dividend is £1,800, he can take £450 only and the balance of £1,350 would be in the Trust Fund."

"These are wonderful rewards for the stockholders," said Grans, "who would have never perceived this. We are getting good dividends at our old age."

"Please give me the name of the beneficiary in each case to register with HMRC," asked Mia.

"There are other small issues, which I will talk to you later about, Mia," said Arun.

Available worldwide from Amazon
and all good bookstores

---

www.mtp.agency

www.facebook.com/mtp.agency

@mtp_agency

Michael Terence
Publishing

www.ingramcontent.com/pod-product-compliance
Lightning Source LLC
LaVergne TN
LVHW091558060526
838200LV00036B/891